The claims of common sense investigates the importance for the social sciences of the ideas developed in Cambridge philosophy between the two World Wars concerning common sense, vague concepts, and ordinary language. John Coates examines the thought of Moore, Ramsey, Wittgenstein, and Keynes, and traces their common drift away from early beliefs about the need for precise concepts and a canonical notation in analysis. He argues that Keynes borrowed from Wittgenstein and Ramsey their reappraisal of vague concepts, and developed the novel argument that when analysing something as complex as social reality, theory might be simplified by using concepts which lack sharp boundaries. Coates then contrasts this conclusion with the view shared by two contemporary philosophical paradigms – formal semantics and Continental post-structuralism – that the vagueness of ordinary language inevitably leads to interpretive indeterminacy. Developing a link between Cambridge philosophy and current work on complexity, vague predicates, and fuzzy logic, he argues that Wittgenstein's and Keynes's ideas on the economy of ordinary language present a mediating route for the social sciences between these philosophical paradigms.

THE CLAIMS OF COMMON SENSE

THE CLAIMS OF
COMMON SENSE

Moore, Wittgenstein, Keynes and the social sciences

JOHN COATES

CAMBRIDGE
UNIVERSITY PRESS

Published by the Press Syndicate of the University of Cambridge
The Pitt Building, Trumpington Street, Cambridge CB2 IRP
40 West 20th Street, New York, NY 10011–4211, USA
10 Stamford Road, Oakleigh, Melbourne 3166, Australia

First published 1996

Printed in Great Britain at the University Press, Cambridge

A catalogue record for this book is available from the British Library

Library of Congress cataloguing in publication data
Coates, J. (John)
The claims of common sense: Moore, Wittgenstein, Keynes and
the social sciences / John Coates
p.   cm.
Includes index.
ISBN 0 521 41256 0
1. Social sciences – Philosophy. 2. Philosophy, English – 20th
century. 1. Title.
H61.C497 1996
300'.1 – dc20   95–34573 CIP

ISBN 0 521 41256 0 hardback

For Sally Carling Coates,
and to the memory of
Margaret Coates

... it is the mark of an educated man to look for precision in each class of things just so far as the nature of the subject admits.

Aristotle,
Nicomachean Ethics

Contents

Preface

As a student of both philosophy and history it was a long time before I noticed the large gulf existing between the philosophies I read and believed and the methods I actually used when researching concrete historical questions. It has taken a lot of effort since that time to bring my two interests into closer proximity. A big part of the problem was the shortage of works on the philosophy of history and the social sciences written by practicing historians and social scientists. This was not always the case. Aristotle, Locke, Hume, Smith, Mill, and Marx all achieved some sort of unity of theory and practice. But during this century, after Weber and Collingwood, the tradition thins out. What emerged in their place were the fundamentalist, proselytizing tracts of positivist philosophers. These tracts were flawed logically and had a paucity of compelling results to offer, but they none the less laid claim to the integrity of the natural sciences. This left many social scientists unconvinced, yet defensive. The only alternative paradigm was that of hermeneutics, but it rested all too often on unstable logical foundations, in particular on untenable distinctions between the natural and social worlds; and it proved weak in practice when the causal chain of events was sought. The gulf between philosophy and the practice of social science and history is today as wide as it ever gets. For the dominant philosophical paradigms with which we are confronted are the formal semantics of analytic philosophy and the textual nihilism of post-structuralism. Philosophically it seems we must chose between an austere and highly inappropriate canonical notation or admit with Derrida that our native intellectual apparatus inevitably leads us into paradox and confusion. I, like many others, refuse to accept that these alternatives map out our true situation. In between these unpalatable choices there are the common sense practices of researching scholars, practices that are characterized at their best by clear prose and compelling argumentation. Such tools are marked by vagueness and may harbour the truth-value gaps feared by formal semantics, but they are none the less capable of discovery, theoretical elegance, and persuasion.

In attempting to discover the philosophical merits of methods I naturally used and trusted, I gravitated towards pragmatism and the tradition of common sense philosophers, in particular the later ones such as Peirce and Popper. Both schools have worked to liberalize our conceptions of rational procedure. However, within these traditions the most important work for my purposes was that done in Cambridge between the Wars, by G. E. Moore, Frank Ramsey, Ludwig Wittgenstein, and John Maynard Keynes. The drift away from the canonical notation of analytic philosophy and logical atomism towards an analysis of vague concepts led to some surprising conclusions concerning the theoretical merits of ordinary language. While analytic philosophers such as Russell, and today Quine, argue that simplification of theory is best served by admitting entities with clear identity conditions, it is possible that the complexity of social phenomena might best be handled by vague concepts, or what Crispin Wright has termed "tolerant" concepts. In this case simplification of theory is advanced by concepts lacking sharp boundaries. The core of this argument was worked out by Wittgenstein, but it was carried into the social sciences by Keynes. There are some startling passages in Keynes's manuscripts from the thirties which indicate that he had been involved with the issue. It turns out that he was in close collaboration with Wittgenstein during the period in which Wittgenstein was discovering the challenge which vague concepts posed for analytic philosophy. Part of the book therefore focuses on Keynes's case for the utility of tolerant concepts in the social sciences. I should point out, however, that my interest in Keynes does not derive from a concern for the methodology of economics. I am not an economist, and I have a poor understanding of the work being done at the forefront of that subject. Keynes is important to the issue at hand because he is one of the few philosophers to have worked out the implications for the social sciences of Wittgenstein's views on vagueness.

The philosophical work on vague concepts thus permits some sort of philosophical defense of the common sense practices of presently unreformulated, qualitative social science and history. It is an argument for the utility of vague concepts in the social sciences that is developed in this book. In the literature on the subject, beginning with Sidgwick and Peirce, running through Cambridge philosophy, and continuing up to the work on fuzzy logic today, I have found the beginnings of a philosophical position which takes a step towards closing the gap, in my mind at any rate, between the theory and practice of social research.

I have over the years pestered many busy people for advice and criticism, and have benefited greatly from their pointing out countless obvious and not-so-obvious errors. Those that remain are, of course, entirely my responsibility. Thanks, with all the provisos, to Michael Nedo, Rhush Rhees, Alice Ambrose, Gay Meeks, Christopher Ricks, Stephen Toulmin, Christopher Hookway, Geoff Harcourt, John Mighton, Sunil Khilnani, Rebecca Wilson, Brian Pedersen, and James Birch. I have been particularly buoyed by encouragement and advice from Geoffrey Hawthorn, for which I am most grateful.

Unpublished writings of J. M. Keynes are the copyright of The Provost and Scholar of King's College, Cambridge 1995. I wish to thank Jane Burch for permission to quote from the unpublished correspondence of Frank Ramsey.

My research was funded by grants from the British Council and the Social Sciences and Humanities Research Council of Canada. I am extremely grateful for the opportunities these organizations afforded me.

Introduction

Philosophical talk of common sense involves us in a contradiction. The notion points to an inchoate body of beliefs which form the background to our intellectual activities, both high and low. This inherited wisdom is commonly seen as the first line of defense against cranks, and the counter-intuitiveness of new ideas is considered a valued spur to further scrutiny. Common sense is like the loyal opposition in parliamentary democracies – annoying in its constant criticism and in the inertia it adds to the intellectual enterprise, yet important over the long haul in catching unnoticed error. This is, one might say, the common sense understanding of common sense. But philosophy traditionally has attempted to bring our intellectual activities within the purview of a transparent rationality, with the goal usually of improving the idioms if not the content of these activities; and a realm of inchoate and inertial beliefs has been anathema to that project. Perhaps that is why historically philosophers have been so impatient in listening to the claims which common sense has in formulating and justifying our beliefs; next to Plato's or Descartes's ideal knowledge it merited as little respect as folklore. This was certainly the reaction of many when the concept was made a philosophical term of trade. Thomas Reid, for example, and later G. E. Moore, took common sense to consist of a body of indubitable and natural beliefs, and on the basis of this view argued that the skeptical conclusions implied by empiricist epistemology were parasitic upon the forms of belief it doubts. Kant for one was unimpressed with this line of argument, and attacked the intellectual Luddism of the Scottish School: "To appeal to common sense when insight and science fail ... this is one of the subtle discoveries of modern times, by means of which the most superficial ranter can safely enter the lists with the most thorough thinker and hold his own."[1] Kant's words have an echo today, for to many the concept smacks of Anglo nostalgia for a less specialized time, an era when the ideal of the amateur seemed a noble ideal to pursue, and the approach of muddling through the only sound one to follow. Appeals to the notion are often seen as reactionary and irresponsible obstacles to the advancement of learning; common sense, according to this interpretation, is not a repository of collective wisdom, it is coextensive with the corpus of past errors.

Much philosophy since the time of Nietzsche and Wittgenstein has abandoned the reconstructive ambitions of traditional philosophy and has therefore been more generous in its appraisal of common sense. However, the conflict between the vagueness of common sense and everyday language and the demands of theory re-emerge. Today few philosophers argue for an indubitable faculty of intuition, and the most influential account of common sense derives from Otto Neurath's metaphor: common sense and ordinary language are like a boat we must rebuild plank by plank while remaining afloat in it. Common sense is not a timeless body of truths, it is merely the current state of theory, our inevitable starting-points for further research, starting-points moreover from which we slowly evolve. This account retains the critical function common sense has always played in philosophy as it implies that skepticism begs the question it raises; and it argues against the more ambitious philosophical projects of a blanket revision of our thought – we have no point outside of common sense from which to remake our conceptual world. Neurath's metaphor is invoked by many different schools of thought who are in other ways in substantial disagreement, but this shared recognition of our starting-points in common sense masks a widespread doubt as to the seaworthiness of the boat in the first place. Indeed, two of the most influential research programs in the philosophical world today, the formal semantics of analytic philosophy, on the one hand, and post-structuralism, on the other, in most ways antithetical to each other, share a fundamental belief in the untrustworthiness of common sense and ordinary language.

[1] *Prolegomena to Any Future Metaphysics*, edited by Lewis White Beck (Indianapolis: Bobbs-Merrill for the Library of Liberal Arts, 1950), p. 7.

This shared starting-point is found in the thought of their founding fathers, Frege, Russell, and Tarski, on the one hand, and Marx, Freud, and Nietzsche, on the other. Tarski, for example, argued that ordinary language is semantically closed and therefore that it leads to antinomies; it is contradictory. As such it is unsuited for philosophical analysis. He sought recourse in the language of a formal semantics. Today, many working within the paradigm established by Frege, Russell, and Tarski similarly find natural language riddled with defects which prevent the construction of a fully extensional language. The problem is that idioms employing tense, quotation, modalities, and talk of intentions lead to referentially opaque contexts. Particularly troublesome in this regard is the inevitable vagueness of ordinary concepts; for quantification to proceed we require entities with clear identity conditions, something which vagueness prevents. Thus, many in the analytic tradition, and Quine is a good example here, accept Neurath's metaphor, but quickly leave common sense behind in their construction of a canonical notation that involves a drastic reparsing of the idioms of natural language.

This distrust of common sense is not confined to analytic philosophy. On the Continent we find a very different sort of criticism being voiced by the post-structuralists, but one that shares with formal semantics a belief in the vagueness and contradiction that ordinary language harbours. Derrida, currently the most influential of that school, has produced a dizzying form of philosophical reading designed to show the impossibility of univocal meaning. Wedding Saussures structural linguistics with Nietzsche's account of the pervasive metaphoricity of language, Derrida has tried to show that symbols are understood only within a network of differences from other symbols; they contain nothing within themselves which might be grasped as their meaning. On the basis of this insight he launched an assault on the entire history of the "philosophy of presence" which, he claims, has been dominated by the mistaken belief that forms, ideas, or meanings can be immediately intuited. His almost narcotic deconstructive analysis involves showing how concepts melt in our hands, dissolve into their other, and undermine our assumed belief in understanding and reason. Where we thought there was serious thought, we now find only the freeplay of metaphorical *jouissance*.

Post-structuralism and analytic philosophy thus, ironically, share a common starting-point – a belief that the vagueness of ordinary language inevitably leads us astray. The dominant philosophical paradigms in the English-speaking world and the Continent differ characteristically in that the former sees our salvation in the ascent to a rarified, Apollonian realm of formal semantics, while the latter recommends a descent into the Dionysian underworld of metaphor. These alternatives are the philosophical gamut that common sense must run today.

They are also the ones which map out the methodological possibilities for the social sciences. Positivism in its various incarnations has for a long time led social scientists to emulate the methods of the natural sciences, Newtonian mechanics in particular. The endeavor has been underwritten at different times by various beliefs: the ontological belief that humans too are matter in motion; the methodological belief that only experimental or deductive science can lead us out of the babel of opinions that clutter the market-place; the belief that a science of intention is impossible; and the current belief in formal semantics that only a canonical notation patterned on the language of physics can close the truth-value gaps existing in ordinary language. For these various reasons many analytic philosophers of the social sciences find the rhetorical practices of many of the liberal arts pre-scientific. Doubt has also been thrown on them by post-structural thought on the subject. Derrida argues that the attempt to elaborate concepts for social analysis is doomed to a fate of paradox and self-delusion. Michel Foucault sees social discourse masking power relations within society; the Marxists find discourse inevitably reflecting class position; and Lacanian Freudians too argue that surface thought conceals deeper concerns. For all these thinkers our common sense understanding of what is taking place on the surface of thought is an illusion.

Thus in both philosophy and the social sciences we are faced with two daunting paradigms: one which finds a properly founded discourse only in the language of physics, and the other which argues that social theory inevitably trades in illusions, ones masking either conceptual contradiction or class interests. Common sense reactions have occurred in philosophy when too many of our natural idioms, forms of argument, or beliefs have been challenged by a new paradigm. When Dr. Johnson kicked his stone he demonstrated that his native belief in physical objects was stronger than any epistemological argument Berkeley had to offer. And Reid drew the line when Hume cast doubt on our ability to know the objects of perception and on the possibility of disinterested moral acts. Of course others, also in the name of common sense, refused to believe that the world was not flat. There is indeed a difference between these cases and to maintain it we need not rely on a categorical distinction between science and philosophy. It is not the case that common sense has an authority in philosophy that it does not have in science. Common sense merely points to the rational procedure of tenaciously holding on to our current beliefs until enough evidence is mustered to warrant their abandonment. It is a question of degree. From this perspective science has fully warranted a constant throwing off of the old, and epistemological theory has never managed to achieve such a consensus. Moreover, the inertia of common sense has proven valuable in philosophy as we now recognize that empiricist epistemology rested on a naive view as to the possibility of isolating sense data independently of a conceptual framework; in this Johnson and Reid were right – a belief in objects is logically prior to talk of sensation. The same can be said for the reluctance of many in the social sciences and humanities to discard rhetorical forms of discourse: positivist, semantic, and post-structuralist theories have not offered enough in the way of theoretical simplification or empirical result to warrant an abandonment of our intuitions concerning the methods appropriate for these fields. Furthermore, many reject the view that the results of presently unreformulated fields such as history and political theory are undisciplined, emotive arm-waving. There is today something of a common sense reaction to the intellectual alternatives presented to us by formal semantics and post-structuralism. Many philosophers, critics, and social scientists do not accept the terms of the intellectual landscape, that we have to choose between an unattainable rationality and none at all. There is a middle route between these paradigms, and it is displayed in the common sense of those social scientists and critics who have resisted the pull of currently influential philosophies. If common sense is understood as the current state of theory, then for a wide spectrum of disciplines within the humanities and social sciences this involves a methodological ideal of clear prose and persuasive argumentation. And the scholars conducting concrete research in these fields refuse to concede that their efforts can be dismissed as pre-scientific or pre-post-modern.[2]

It is with a philosophical examination of the claims of this common sense that I am concerned. The alternatives presented today between the restrictive rationalism of much analytic philosophy and the anti-rationalism of post-structuralism is an inaccurate description of our intellectual situation. Ordinary language and rhetorical skills may indeed fall short of the Platonic, Cartesian, or Quinean epistemic ideals, but that does not mean that we are left with a global failure of meaning, as the post-structuralists imply. Thinkers who take common sense seriously do not believe that the failure of our language to meet the demands of extensionalism leaves us in any sort of crisis. Our true situation has been incisively depicted by the literary critic Christopher Ricks. In the course of discussing deconstruction, he considers the idea that "nothing is certain, determinate, stable" and Derrida's resulting "thrilled insistence that *reading* is impossible":

All that is necessary is to define reading as something that reading has never been thought to be (absolutely entire, absolutely indubitable), and presto, you've added to the human stock of impossibilities – always terrifically cheering, since impossibilities are so much easier to live with than difficulties.[3]

It has often occurred in philosophy that reason has been so narrowly defined that it is found to be useless for most of the questions we ask, and thus an irrationalism or mysticism has emerged as an antidote. Our real situation involves neither; it involves rather, as Ricks puts it, difficulties. Our ordinary language and rhetorical skills may not meet the demands of Quine's canonical notation, but they do not leave us hopelessly tangled in a web of metaphoricity. Historical and literary interpretation inevitably leave doubts, and unanimity and certainty are rarely if ever attained in these fields. But

---

[2] A good sample statement of this reaction is found in *Plausible Worlds*, by Geoffrey Hawthorn (Cambridge University Press, 1991). He develops an analysis of possibility in the social sciences and concludes that "were it not that 'commonsense' has acquired a bad name in what may loosely be thought of as theoretical argument, I would be tempted to say that against both the old defenders of theoretical reason in the human sciences and their modernist critics, I am merely insisting that we take our commonsensical experience of the human world seriously" p. 185.

[3] "Princes of the Mental States, Review of Giles Gunn, The Culture of Criticism and the Criticism of Culture," in *The New York Times Review of Books*, May 14, 1987.

these characteristics of inquiry point out its everyday difficulties, not the impossibility of inquiry under present methods.

This is not to say that Tarski and Derrida have been wrong about the occasional inconsistency of ordinary language. But a recognition of the phenomena they have pointed out should not be seen as implying the need for a flight to formal semantics or a poetry of word association. Tarski's antinomies were often drawn from trivial examples that do little to warrant the abandonment of ordinary language.[4] And it does not make sense to say, as Derrida seems to, that there is a global failure of meaning. We should be wary of such generalizations. There may be utterances, passages, or historical events which admit contradictory interpretations. But the answer to this problem is either to live with a range of possible interpretations, or, in the case of an utterance, to ask the speaker what he means, ask him to clear up the misunderstanding. Perhaps we could continue this interrogation in Socratic style until the speaker is dumbfounded. But to press the questioning beyond a certain point, and that point will depend on the question at hand, is not a display of philosophical ingenuity; it is merely pedantic. The difficulties which we face under present methods do not stem from a defect in our tools. They are not philosophically interesting problems; they are nothing more, but then nothing less, than the ongoing difficulties of discussion and interpretation. Recognizing the pitfalls in discourse highlighted by Tarski and Derrida is an invitation to examine the particular cases where communication fails, and to assess how best to clear up the misunderstanding.

One way to broker the differences existing between the dominant philosophical paradigms and common sense is to re-examine the role of vague concepts in social research. For both Derrida and Quine, who I take to be influential representatives of their fields, vagueness is a defect in language which issues in interpretive indeterminacy. This view lies at the heart of our current problem. However, there is a growing body of work, beginning with the later

---

[4] See Avrum Stroll, "Is Everyday Language Inconsistent?" *Mind* 63 (1954), pp. 219–25. Stroll admits that we can invent situations in which self-referential sentences lead to contradiction, but in order to draw the lesson from these artificial circumstances that Tarski does "we must be shown that natural languages are inconsistent in the stronger sense that *in fact* such self-referential sentences do or will occur in the common use of these languages" (p. 222). Stroll illustrates through a few examples how unlikely this is.

Wittgenstein, which provides grounds for believing this view to be wrong. Wittgenstein, Max Black, Crispin Wright, and the theorists of fuzzy logic, to name a few, have shown that language is, relative to a Fregean ideal, inescapably vague. That observation at the least makes formal semantics look difficult. Russell pointed out the pervasive vagueness of words, but none the less combined this view with formal semantics by arguing that language only gets what meaning it does attain by approaching the ideal language of logical atomism. However, a more fruitful approach is to work in the opposite direction, by examining the ways in which vagueness may be a virtue in serving the purposes language must serve. It all depends on the function of the tool at hand: sometimes a blurred picture may communicate more meaning than a sharp one. The particular linguistic tool with which I am concerned is the language or languages of the social sciences. And here theoretical simplification of as complex a phenomena as social reality may be advanced, rather than impeded, by concepts which are tolerant of borderline cases. This is an argument that I have extracted from Cambridge philosophy between the Wars, and to do so I have followed several threads leading up to it: G. E. Moore's defense of common sense, Frank Ramsey's and Ludwig Wittgenstein's analysis of vagueness, and Keynes's application of these ideas to the social sciences. Keynes's contribution warrants a close examination. He had occasion to discuss the problems of formalization with Wittgenstein, and what resulted in their later philosophies is a compelling argument which points to a mediating route between the philosophical paradigms which today define our intellectual condition. Whereas formal semantics and post-structuralism see vagueness as an impediment to theoretical work, Keynes saw it as an essential property of the language of social science. Formalization of even a part of what goes into our common sense understanding of society would be, as he said, "prolix and complicated to the point of obscurity." Theories constructed with vague concepts paradoxically can maximize precision and economy. For Quine, theoretical simplification is achieved through formalization; for Keynes, it is attained through the concepts of ordinary discourse. Such an argument goes a long way towards vindicating the common sense of many forms of social interpretation currently under suspicion of being methodologically behind the times.

COUNSELS OF PRUDENCE

Methodology has commonly been seen as providing us with a rule book for rational procedure to follow if it is to discover the way the world is, according to an ontology, or if it is to emulate the patently successful methods of the natural sciences. It is difficult today in light of the prevailing skepticism concerning the claims of ontology and epistemology to promote a single, objective, and ahistorical method. Languages are more persuasively defended, on pragmatic grounds, by their proven utility in handling the questions posed. According to this line of reasoning, methodology is no longer seen as providing universal constraints on rational procedure, but rather with "counsels of prudence," as John Dunn calls them, i.e. practical advice on how best to solve a particular problem under study.[5] The value of these rules is proved in practice, not in an a priori manner. The place to look for valuable methodological insights therefore is not in the writings of logicians, but in the practice of successful social scientists. They are the ones with advice to give. The later philosophical writings of Keynes provide a remarkable discussion of language in the social sciences which addresses the issues raised here. Since he was such an important social theorist, Keynes's methodological comments are not empty dictums on how things should be done. He was also an accomplished philosopher who understood the problems of epistemology and method which were to occupy philosophy up to this day. Indeed, Keynes was aware of the tendencies in twentieth century-thought towards either a restrictive scientism or an irrationalist alternative; and he understood the risks they posed for ethical, political, and social thought. Much of his later philosophical writings focused on the inappropriate emulation of the methods of the natural sciences. But he also had occasion to comment on the other risk to reasonable thought marked out by the precursors of post-structuralism. He must have been aware of the creeping doubt these theorists of suspicion were sowing as he lamented that the world had earlier breathed "a purer, sweeter air by far than Freud cum Marx."[6] His ideas on language,

[5] "Practising History and Social Science on 'Realist' Assumptions," in *Political Obligation in its Historical Context. Essays in Political Theory* (Cambridge University Press, 1980), p. 111.

[6] *Collected Works*, vol. 10, p. 442. I find this passage surprising in its prescience as the synthesis of Marx and Freud really did not pick up steam until the time of Marcuse. All references to the work of Keynes will be to *The Collected Works of John Maynard Keynes*,

together with those of the other Cambridge philosophers, continue
to offer a viable alternative to today's paradigms.

In chapter 1 I survey the history of the notion of common sense in
philosophy, paying particular attention to how the logic of vagueness emerged as an integral part of its analysis. This is the focus of
the book, so the bulk of the philosophers I examine are from the
English-speaking world. My goal is to argue for a mediating path
between formal semantics and post-structuralism, but the bulk of
the book concentrates on the former tradition. I briefly return
in the conclusion to discuss the post-structuralists. But my main
concern is to trace the evolution of issues concerning common
sense, everyday language, and vagueness, and these have been
more extensively dealt with within Anglo-Saxon philosophy. The
survey of common sense in the first part of the chapter sets the
stage for a more focused examination of a tension existing within
the thought of Quine, between his recognition of our inevitable
starting-points in common sense and his rapid departure from
these starting-points as he moves on to defend his canonical
notation. I focus on Quine because he is such an influential figure
in formal semantics, and because he writes of the conflicting
attractions of common sense and an ideal language in such a
candid and exciting way. The story of this conflict is continued
in chapter 2 where I turn back in time to show how the same
forces molded Cambridge philosophy during the thirties. Here
Wittgenstein takes center stage, for he fought the same battle
Quine was to face later on, although Wittgenstein took the opposite
route in that he abandoned the ideal language of logical atomism in
favor of preserving the vagueness of ordinary language.

In chapters 3 and 4 I weave Keynes into the fabric of these
debates by showing how he belonged to the Cambridge philosophical scene and how he evolved with it. Cambridge philosophy
during the twenties and thirties was the scene of some very intense
and fruitful discussions between Moore, Russell, and Wittgenstein,
as well as the economist-philosophers Piero Sraffa and Ramsey. It
has not been appreciated that Keynes was also an integral member
of this group, and kept his finger on the pulse of the new ideas. I try
to reconstruct parts of these discussions and to display Keynes's

edited by D. E. Moggridge and E. Johnson (London: Macmillan for the Royal Economic
Society).

participation in them by tracing the development of a few issues in analytic philosophy such as the analysis of vague concepts, and the notion of an ideal language. Attention will also be paid to the influence exerted on the evolution of Cambridge philosophy by Moore. Indeed, I think much of Cambridge philosophy, both early and late, can be seen as shifting attitudes towards Moore's persuasive defense of common sense, as this set up a dynamic contradiction between those philosophies which suggested the need for a reconstruction of our language and those that found it in order as it is. Keynes was caught between these movements in his early work, trying to extend Russell's logic so that it encompassed Moore's common sense. This set up an ambivalent attitude toward analytic philosophy and made it difficult for Keynes to come down squarely in favor of analysis or common sense and ordinary language. However, in his later work he clearly takes the second approach, not only explicitly in his methodological writings, but also implicitly in the language used in writing his masterpiece, *The General Theory of Employment, Interest and Money*. In the early thirties he confessed to Roy Harrod that he was "returning to an age-long tradition of common sense."[7] In his manuscripts from the time we find a developed argument for the case that vague concepts, the concepts of ordinary discourse, contribute to the simplification of social theory. Keynes's views on the nature of the concepts required for theoretical work, at least within the social sciences, are thus set up as a counter-argument to Quine's case for a canonical notation.

Wittgenstein and Keynes understood concepts to be samples rather than generalizations. In chapter 5 I look at the argument that models in the social sciences as well should be viewed as samples. Keynes again bulks large in this argument. In developing it he drew a distinction between the natural and the social sciences; and in so doing he skirted around several familiar positions, such as the hermeneutic case for adequacy, but deftly avoided the onto-logical and methodological traps which often limit their appeal. His choice of a language different than those of the natural sciences turns on a recognition of the complexity of social phenomena; concepts that are tolerant of borderline cases facilitate efficiency of theory and communication. His case is pragmatic rather than ontological. In other words, he does not argue that it is necessarily

---

[7] *Collected Works*, vol. 13, p. 552.

the case that the social sciences use the concepts of ordinary discourse and models resembling somewhat ideal types. Rather, given that the causal factors at work, in macro-economics at any rate, are often historically specific institutions, and that market expectations are chaotic, it is best not to stray too far from concepts and mental constructs with which we have an immediate understanding. If we sever this connection we'll be adrift in confusion. However, for other questions it may well turn out that formalized theory is preferable.[8]

Chapter 6 is somewhat tangential to the issue at hand, for I there sketch a biographical picture of the Cambridge philosophical community. Keynes's interpretation of the ideas being developed in Cambridge bulks large in my argument and I would prefer to present this argument and then move on. But, since it is a somewhat new reading of Keynes, I must assemble the biographical details of his friendships with Moore, Wittgenstein, Ramsey, and Sraffa in order to show that the textual similarities between Keynes's philosophical writings from the thirties and those of Wittgenstein and Ramsey were the natural products of a closer collaboration than has been supposed. The chapter may be a detour, but what emerges as an externality, so to speak, is a missing chapter in the story of Keynes's life as well as in the history of Cambridge philosophy.

In the conclusion I return to contemporary philosophy with the ideas extracted from early Cambridge philosophy and insert them into current discussions of vague concepts and fuzzy logic. I there address the criticisms voiced by positivism and formal semantics that a theory employing the concepts of ordinary discourse is necessarily unsystematic and undisciplined. I also face the concerns of Continental philosophers that such a form of social theory necessarily fossilizes current beliefs and prejudices. I will not deny that this is always a risk; it may even be a prevalent outcome. But the answer to the problem is one that is handled within our native theory, not by a flight to a new level of discourse. Furthermore, the problem must be occasional, rather than permanent, otherwise

---

[8] Keynes's vision of a social reality characterized by phase changes and emergent properties has been more fully developed recently by the theorists of complexity at the Santa Fe Institute. I do not develop the comparison in this book, but it is worth noting that Keynes's later philosophy of the social sciences addresses many of the questions raised by the theorists of complexity.

the criticism loses its validity. As Donald Davidson has shown, we can make no sense out of the idea that all our beliefs can be wrong. Analogously, it is untenable to argue that there is always a failure of meaning, or that all our views mask self-interest.

One of the questions raised in the book but left unanswered stems from the conclusion that the language appropriate for a social science will depend on the purpose it serves. Crispin Wright, for one, argues that the vagueness we find in ordinary language results from the coarse role these concepts have to play.[9] To extend this argument into the social sciences raises the monumental question of the purposes of the social sciences. I cannot begin to handle such a large issue, as by the nature of the case it would involve analyzing not only each one of the social sciences, but each branch of them as well. But the argument derived from Cambridge philosophy, and from Keynes in particular, none the less helps answer the analytic and post-structuralist critics who have penned blanket methodological critiques of the value of theoretical work conducted by means of rhetorical tools. The conclusion I draw concerning the respectability of these methods may lack the subtlety of a case by case analysis of the use of concepts in the different social sciences, but then so too do the criticisms I attempt to answer. Besides, an anomalous observation is sufficient to falsify an hypothesis, and the success of Keynes's approach is enough to cast doubt on the truth of the theories now dominating the philosophical world.

---

[9] "On the Coherence of Vague Predicates," *Synthese* 30 (1975), pp. 336–7.

CHAPTER I

A short history of common sense

DR. JOHNSON'S TRADITION

Aristotle's careful attention to, and respect for, common forms of speech makes him the first of the common sense philosophers. However, if we concentrate on modern philosophy, we can begin with the not-too-surprising point that common sense became a topic of philosophical importance when it was challenged in a concerted manner. Descartes did this by arguing that all we believe is subject to doubt until set upon a foundation of clear and distinct ideas, which he took to be the geometric properties of matter. The empiricists also sought secure starting-points for knowledge, but found them instead in the givens of sensation. Neither of these philosophical movements welcomed the skeptical conclusions many drew from their ideas; rationalists and empiricists had the more laudable goal of redirecting philosophy towards the methods of deductive and experimental science. But the problem they introduced into philosophy was the difficult one of finding a way out from the contents of consciousness to the external world; and the difficulty of doing so led to various skeptical conclusions being drawn. The empiricist epistemology inevitably seemed to invite a solipsism of the present moment. Berkeley was read as arguing that matter did not exist, that the only reality to material objects lay in their being perceived. Hume did not go as far as to deny the existence of the objects that cause sensation, but claimed that all we could know were the sensations. These empiricist philosophies were largely responsible for the rise of a school of common sense. However, much of the common sense reaction to empiricism can be found in Hume's own writings, as he had a characteristically complex attitude to skepticism. He did indeed claim that we are in contact only with the contents of consciousness, that the self is nothing more than this stream of sensation, and that reason is incapable of justifying our beliefs about causation or moral intuitions. At the same time he fully recognized the difficulty of living in accordance with these views, and in a famous passage he tells how his doubts are dispersed by falling back into the flow of life:

Most fortunately it happens, that since reason is incapable of dispelling these clouds, nature herself suffices to that purpose, and cures me of this philosophical melancholy and delirium . . . I dine, I play a game of back-gammon, I converse, and am merry with my friends; and when after three or four hour's amusement, I wou'd return to these speculations, they appear so cold, and strain'd, and ridiculous, that I cannot find in my heart to enter into them any farther . . . Here then I find myself absolutely and necessarily determin'd to live, and talk, and act like other people in the common affairs of life.[1]

Hume's predicament nicely illustrates how philosophy since his time has been pulled between the view that thought is most securely founded on a bedrock of indubitable intuitions, and one that sees our starting-points as inescapably anchored in the more mundane givens of common sense and the life-world. In fact his account of the solace received from everyday life was itself to anticipate the critique voiced by most common sense philosophers – that skepticism is parasitic upon the forms of belief it calls in question.

Samuel Johnson was the first to put the boot to empiricism in the name of common sense. But his defiant kicking of the stone did little to challenge the new epistemology. A more concerted attempt came from Thomas Reid and the school he established, the Scottish School of common sense. Reid spoke of common sense as an amorphous body of ill-defined, yet self-evident, principles which guide our judgment in the normal course of life. They are ill-defined because they are habitual and pervasive; we become aware of them only when they are challenged, as they were by empiricism. However, once brought to our attention they are seen as the most obvious truths: the self-evident "is the province, and the sole province, of common sense."[2] This double nature of the specific

---

[1] *A Treatise of Human Nature*, 2nd edn edited by L. A. Selby-Bigge (Oxford: Clarendon, 1978), p. 269.
[2] *Philosophical Works*, vol. 1, edited by William Hamilton (Hildesheim: Verlagsbuchhand-lung, 1967), p. 425.

principles is also characteristic of the definition of common sense itself: in an analysis which sounds very Wittgensteinian to us today, he said of the concept that

men may agree in the meaning of the word who have different opinions about (its) limits, or who even never thought of fixing them. This is as intelligible as, that all Englishmen should mean the same thing by the county of York, though perhaps not a hundredth part of them can point out its precise limits . . . Indeed, it seems to me, that common sense is as unambiguous a word and as well understood as the county of York.[3]

This realm of common knowledge is presupposed by our actions and beliefs, as it is by philosophy. The propositions of common sense attain a certainty no philosophical argument can match, so the idea of the latter casting doubt on the former is backwards; we have nothing more fundamental to work with than common sense. Modern philosophy has characteristically accorded epistemology logical priority over our everyday beliefs. But if we consider the two competing claims "There is a desk in front of me" and "We have knowledge only of our sensations, not of material objects," we must conclude that the former attains a certainty the latter lacks. This is an argument shared by most philosophies of common sense. But despite its force epistemology has dominated philosophy until this century.

Reid employed this gambit against Hume and Berkeley when he claimed that we are unable to doubt propositions such as our acts of perception assume the existence of independently existing objects; there is a self separable from the stream of sensation; every event necessarily has a cause and an effect; and finally we are capable of making moral judgments which are independent of judgments of our own interests. To press his point Reid appealed to the Hume who has left his study and rejoined society, for when philosophers "condescend to mingle again with the human race, and to converse with a friend, a companion, or a fellow-citizen, the ideal system vanishes; common sense, like an irresistible torrent, carries them along; and, in spite of all their reasoning and philosophy, they believe their own existence, and the existence of other things."[4] Reid thus argued that a philosopher should maintain consistency between his ideas and common sense; he should make sure that his

---

[3] Ibid., p. 423. Compare *Philosophical Investigations*, sects. 68 and 99.   [4] Ibid., p. 110.

system is not contradicted by his own habitual beliefs and forms of inference. Failure to do so produces paradox, and Reid took the ridiculousness of a conclusion to be a clue that it is wrong; he made frequent use, as Sidgwick pointed out, of the *argumentum ad risum*,[5] playfully suggesting that a skeptic's argument is like a hobby-horse – harmless if ridden in a closet, "but, if he should take him abroad with him to church . . . his heir would immediately call a jury, and seize his estate."[6]

If Reid's philosophy embodies the basic argument used by most later philosophers who resorted to a defense by common sense, it also contained many of the problems. To begin with, if common sense is understood as opinions and principles of judgment shared by all people, then is there a role for the philosopher? Reid at times argued as if he believed that the man on the street is as competent a judge of these issues as any academic. But this conclusion is unnecessary, for just because we all share certain elementary beliefs and forms of speech it does not follow that we are equally capable of describing these things.[7] None the less there remains something odd about a specialist in common sense. Related to this is the seeming absurdity of arguments within common sense: what do we do in cases of dispute about what common sense has to say on a subject? Reid thought this was a groundless worry because "truth will always be consistent with itself."[8] But in this connection it is worth remembering that Berkeley himself continually appealed to the "common sense and natural notions of mankind";[9] by so doing he made the point that the notion of a material object is a philosophical notion, not one found in common usage. So here we have a case of conflicting claims for the mantle of common sense. There is also the issue as to the types of question on which common sense has a say. Reid resorted to it on questions of broad philosophical concern: are there, for example, objects independent of sensation? But does it have a say in empirical questions? Common sense does

---

[5] In "The Philosophy of Common Sense," *Lectures on the Philosophy of Kant* (London: Macmillan, 1905), p. 414.
[6] *Philosophical Works*, p. 110.
[7] On this point see, for example, William Hamilton, "On the Philosophy of Common Sense," in *The Works of Thomas Reid*, vol. 2, 8th edn (Edinburgh: Maclachlan and Stewart, 1880.), pp. 751–2.
[8] *Philosophical Works*, p. 425.
[9] *Three Dialogues Between Hylas and Philonous* (Indianapolis: Bobbs-Merrill for the Library of Liberal Arts, 1954), p. 6.

seem to have led us correctly during the debate with empiricism;
and Reid's criticism of the notion of a veil of appearances has been
given a more persuasive defense this century by thinkers such as
Wittgenstein and Donald Davidson. But common sense also led us
to believe that the earth was flat. So it is important to distinguish
the role of common sense in philosophical and empirical questions.
Lastly, are common sense beliefs shared by all people at all times?
or are they culturally specific, and undergoing an evolution? Reid
believed, in a manner similar to the later ideas of Peter Strawson,
in the uniformity and timelessness of a core of common beliefs.[10] I
mention these difficulties with the philosophy of common sense
now so that we can trace their evolution to the more interesting
contemporary treatments at the hands of Davidson, Richard Rorty,
and Quine.

    With Sidgwick and C. S. Peirce several of these issues are taken
up. While the Scottish School held that there was a timeless core
of common sense beliefs, these two thinkers saw this core as
undergoing a slow process of evolution due to the progress of
science. More importantly, they saw philosophy as having a role in
criticizing and changing these beliefs. It is for this reason that their
thought, along with that of others such as Karl Popper, is known as
"critical common sense." Sidgwick proposed common sense as the
inevitable starting point for philosophy, but none the less found
its beliefs confused, inconsistent, and vague. It is the task of
philosophers and scientists to bring order here, and Sidgwick
claimed, in a manner later echoed by Quine, that "Common Sense
organised into Science continually at once corrects and confirms
crude Common Sense."[11] This may indeed have been his goal,
but in his ethical thought, where he attempted a synthesis of the
morality of common sense with utilitarianism, he was skeptical of
attempts to give our moral intuitions a more precise formulation.
The reason is that "so long as they are left in the state of somewhat
vague generalities, as we meet them in ordinary discourse, we
are disposed to yield them unquestioning assent, and it may be
fairly claimed that the assent is approximately universal."[12] More
precise statements of these ethical precepts may leave too many

---

10 See *Individuals* (London: Routledge, 1959).
11 "The Philosophy of Common Sense," p. 425.
12 *The Methods of Ethics*, 7th edn (Indianapolis: Hackett, 1981), p. 342.

applications out of account, and the ones they now cover, they do so in a form that no longer receives universal assent. Vagueness, he believed, may thus be an essential property of our fundamental moral intuitions.

Peirce developed this idea further. He held that "the most distinctive character of the Critical Common-sensist, in contrast to the old Scotch philosopher, lies in his insistence that the acritically indubitable is invariably vague."[13] We have a body of beliefs which we are incapable of doubting, but which we are also incapable of stating precisely. The more precise we make these fundamental beliefs the more subject to doubt they become, while in their ill-defined everyday form they attain the certainty of philosophical starting-points. Unanalyzed, their content and implications are so plastic that nothing could falsify or cast doubt upon them. He considered, for example, our belief in the order of nature: "As precisely defined it can hardly be said to be absolutely indubitable considering how many thinkers there are who do not believe it. But who can think that there is *no* order in nature?"[14] Our moral intuitions, being similarly vague, defy precise reformulation. As in empirical questions, doubt on these matters is increased by critical appraisal; however, "a certain vague residuum" always remains, making it impossible to carry out the Cartesian project of radical doubt.[15] This distinguishes common sense beliefs from empirical ones: when doubt arises from a scientific investigation of the latter we may be compelled to abandon the belief, while common sense propositions cannot be doubted despite the most rigorous attempts at disproof. This raises the question of the reasons for holding our original beliefs. We tend to think that there is some reason for holding them, one that we might have lost sight of. But if we consider them closely, said Peirce, we discover that the belief habits have always been with us, unquestioned and foundationless. They are "of the general nature of instincts";[16] alternatively, they are "ultimate premise[s] . . . held without reference to precise proof."[17] The instinctual nature of common sense Peirce shared with the

[13] *Philosophical Writings of Peirce*, edited by Justus Buchler (New York: Dover, 1955), p. 294.

[14] Ibid., p. 296.

[15] Ibid., p. 295.　　[16] Ibid., p. 293.

[17] *The Collected Papers of Charles Sanders Peirce*, vol. 5, edited by C. Hartshorne and P. Weiss (Cambridge, Mass.: Harvard, 1934), para. 515.

Scottish School, but against it he pointed out that man can outgrow the primitive forms of life in which these instincts had their origin. With the development of technology we are put into situations where our ancient beliefs afford us little direction, and in this case criticism is required. However, here I find his account of the role of criticism difficult to square with his view of the relative immobility of these original instincts. He pointed out that according to the Scottish School it was possible to draw up a list of common sense beliefs which "would hold good for the minds of all men from Adam down."[18] He also claimed that "a modern recognition of evolution must distinguish the Critical Common-sensist from the old school."[19] But then he surprises us with the additional claim that his inquiry into the rate of change of these beliefs "shows me that the changes are so slight from generation to generation, though not imperceptible even in that short period" that he will defer to Reid's judgment that there is a "fixed list . . . the same for all men."[20] If this is the case then it is not clear what function criticism is supposed to play, at least as regards the original beliefs of common sense. I will not press the issue, as Peirce has written too little on the subject to clear up the matter.[21] In short, Peirce criticized skepticism and Cartesian doubt along lines which were later taken up by Davidson in his version of radical interpretation: one must begin inquiry on a basis of uncritically accepted truths; we cannot doubt all our beliefs, nor can we make sense of the claim that they may all be false.

This idea has become very influential, its most popular expression being found in the analogy of Neurath's boat. In Popper's words, "we have, as it were, to reform ordinary language while using it, as described by Neurath in his metaphor of the ship we have to rebuild while trying to keep afloat in it. This indeed is the situation of critical common sense, as I see it."[22] Popper too sees

---

[18] *Philosophical Writings*, p. 293.   [19] Ibid., p. 297.

[20] *Collected Papers*, vol. 5, para. 509.

[21] However for a good discussion of the role of criticism in Peirce's philosophy, see Christopher Hookway, "Critical Common-Sensism and Rational Self-Control," *Nous* 24 (1990), pp. 397–411; and his *Peirce* (London: Routledge, 1985), pp. 229–33. Peirce, according to Hookway, believed that rational self control has a role to play in science but not in discussions of "vital questions," which are the sole province of common sense.

[22] *Objective Knowledge* (Oxford: Clarendon, 1972), p. 60.

a continuity between science and philosophy on the one hand, and common sense on the other, the former being *"enlightened common sense."*[23] In relation to the tradition, Popper shares many views: the belief in the impossibility of Cartesian doubt, and in the untenability of the empiricist view that sensation is the source of secure starting-points for thought, a view he derisively termed the bucket theory of the mind. He shares with Reid a realism concerning these matters, but breaks with his predecessors in denying that there is any immediate knowledge of physical objects or the self. We have to learn about these things; knowledge of both physical objects and sensation is something we acquire, not something we intuit. Nor does Popper view common sense as supplying the building blocks of certainty. "The quest for certainty, for a secure basis for knowledge, has to be abandoned."[24] Common sense is the body of beliefs which currently serves its purposes, which has not given us cause for criticism. It is thus not timeless and objective; it is tentative and evolving. For Popper there is no problem to be solved concerning the timeless core of original beliefs; there is just a pragmatic approach to the growth of knowledge. He calls this philosophy Commonsense Realism. It is one that repudiates much of the tradition of epistemology, and it does so without abandoning the notion of truth, or committing Popper to skepticism. Based on Tarski's semantic account of truth, he argues that truth is merely a property of sentences we are willing to assert; we accept a proposition as true if we have reasons for believing it.

With Wittgenstein and Moore the case for common sense becomes closely tied to an analysis of ordinary language. Moore's article "A Defense of Common Sense" presents an argument quite similar to previous defenses, but its atavism shocked the philosophical world at a time when the methods of *Principia Mathematica* were becoming the predominant style of analysis. Moore listed several propositions which are "so universally held that they may, I think, fairly be called the views of Common Sense."[25] He did not spend much time speculating on the evolution of these beliefs, or on the role of criticism in their development, but he indicated enough to suggest a position similar to Peirce's: these beliefs do change, albeit at a glacial pace, and this is all part of the "progress of

---

[23] Ibid., p. 34.   [24] Ibid., p. 37.
[25] *Some Main Problems of Philosophy* (London: George Allen & Unwin, 1953), p. 2.

knowledge."[26] These propositions he found of great philosophical importance both for their positive contribution to our understanding of the most general characteristics of the world, and for the criticism they afford of skepticism and idealism. The list includes such apparent trivialities as that I and other people exist, the world has existed for many years past, there exists a large number of both animate and inanimate objects, material objects exist without being perceived, and so on. He said that propositions such as these are known by all of us with a certainty that skeptical arguments cannot touch. When debating the issue with both empiricists such as Russell and idealists such as Bradley he employed a method he called translation into the concrete.[27] When a philosopher claimed, for example, that there are no material things, Moore took that as implying that there are no hands, and by holding up his hands claimed that we know that at least two material things exist. Similarly with another tenet of empiricism, that we cannot know with certainty any empirical propositions, he merely responded that we know for certain that there is a page in front of us. He lined up his propositions against those of Russell's skeptical empiricism and claimed that he is "*more* certain" of his mundane truths than he is of Russell's epistemology.[28] This is a philosophical gambit we have run across in Reid.

Norman Malcolm has given another interpretation of Moore's argument, one designed to allay the disquieting feeling that Moore is winning his point by begging the question.[29] Like Reid, Malcolm takes Russell's and Bradley's statements as paradoxical, and shocking to a "philosophically unsophisticated person"; they thus "go against 'common sense.'"[30] They do so because they violate ordinary language. These philosophers believe in the need to reformulate ordinary language because it conceals errors, its

---

[26] Ibid., p. 3. For example, he took basic astronomical beliefs to be part of common sense. However, he also pointed out that in more animistic times it was believed that logs and rocks were conscious. p. 8.

[27] "The Conception of Reality," in *Philosophical Studies* (London: Routledge & Kegan Paul, 1922), p. 209.

[28] "Four Forms of Scepticism," in *Philosophical Papers* (London: George Allen & Unwin, 1959), p. 226.

[29] See Alice Ambrose, "Three Aspects of Moore's Philosophy," in *G. E. Moore: Essays in Retrospect* (London: George Allen & Unwin, 1970), pp. 80–8, for a survey of the interpretations and problems of Moore's essay.

[30] "Moore and Ordinary Language," in *The Philosophy of G. E. Moore*, 3rd edn, edited by Paul Arthur Schilpp (La Salle: Open Court, 1968), p. 348.

expressions are self-contradictory. Just as Berkeley thought the notion of a material object was nonsensical, so empiricists such as Russell thought it was not strictly true to say such things as "I see a cat in the tree," or "I know for certain there are several chairs in the room." He thought it more correct to say that when we see a cat we are really seeing part of our brain; and that it is only highly probable that there are chairs in the room, this proposition being a hypothesis. Malcolm interpreted Moore as saying that we cannot be using expressions such as "I know," "I am certain," "I see," incorrectly because they derive their meaning, we learned their use, through precisely the situations to which we are now applying them. Further, if we have a use for the expressions they cannot be self-contradictory because self-contradictory expressions can have no use. In the philosophical literature this has come to be known as the "paradigm case argument." Its opponents, such as John Passmore, simply refuse to accept the implication that philosophers are as bone-headed as to overlook completely the everyday uses of expressions. Morris Lazerowitz has termed this peculiar contradiction between philosophers' professional and everyday beliefs, "Moore's Paradox."[31] One point Passmore presses is that most of the phrases under discussion, such as "material object" and "certainty" are not learned just through humdrum cases; many of them are largely philosophical terms. "Our parents say to us: 'Bring me a chair,' 'Bring me a book,' but never 'Bring me a material thing.'"[32] We first encounter the expression as a philosophical term of trade. Passmore thus sides with Berkeley in believing that revisionary talk of material objects involves no violation of ordinary beliefs.

I will not go into Wittgenstein's philosophy here because he, along with Moore, is dealt with at length in the next chapter. Suffice it for the moment to say that his concern during his later period with ordinary language has much in common with the ideas of the philosophers of common sense. While he distanced himself from Moore's account of common sense, his refrains that in philosophy "we must stick to the subjects of our every-day thinking,"[33]

---

[31] "Moore's Paradox," in *The Philosophy of G. E. Moore* , edited by Schilpp, pp. 369–94.
[32] *Philosophical Reasoning* (New York: Charles Scribner's Sons, 1961), p. 115.
[33] *Philosophical Investigations*, 2nd edn, trans. G. E. M. Anscombe (Oxford: Basil Blackwell, 1958), sect. 106.

and that "what *we* do is bring words back from their metaphysical to their everyday use"[34] are of a piece with the intentions of many of the philosophers we have surveyed. And Wittgenstein too put an analysis of vagueness at the heart of his *Investigations*.

The problem with surveying the history of common sense in philosophy from here is that up to this point it has been like following a river, a single line of thinkers, but after the later Wittgenstein the river spans out into a delta. Based on the work of Wittgenstein, Moore, and John Austin, many contemporary philosophers, such as Strawson, Searle, and Grice, believe an adequate account of meaning must take its start from the acts of everyday language usage. However, it is not only these communication-intention theorists who take common sense seriously, for even theorists of formal semantics such as Quine feel the need to begin their work with a recognition of the common sense within which we find ourselves. Indeed, so pervasive is this concern that it may be questioned whether common sense remains a meaningful criterion for distinguishing parties in the philosophical debates today.[35] Common sense became an issue largely because of the skeptical and reductionist implications of the distinctly modern problematic of epistemology, and of empiricism in particular. Rorty has argued recently that a broad spectrum of post-positivist philosophers has repudiated the epistemological problematic. If such is the case then in one way common sense has carried the day. Perhaps that is why so few philosophers now employ the term. Rorty's synthesis of a large number of recent thinkers, ranging from Wittgenstein and Heidegger, through Davidson and Quine, to Derrida and Foucault certainly suggests that today many of us are, in this limited sense of being anti-epistemology at any rate, commonsensists. It seems that epistemology and common sense wax and wane together as subjects of philosophical concern.

There is indeed some truth to this interpretation of the evolution of the concept of common sense, but I do not believe it has lost its critical function. There is still a broad divide in contemporary philosophy between what one might call revisionists and conservatives, but the locus of debate is no longer specific metaphysical

---

[34] Ibid., 116.
[35] Strawson, however, does see it as the central fault line in contemporary philosophy. See "Meaning and Truth," in *Logico-Linguistic Papers* (London: Methuen, 1971).

beliefs, as it is the status of the idioms and forms of argumentation used in methodologically unreformulated disciplines such as history, ethics, literary criticism, and the social sciences. Many philosophers indeed take their start from the givens of natural language rather than from sense data or rationalist intuitions, but it is common to find this level of discourse defective. Philosophers of both formal semantics and post-structuralism share the belief that ordinary language is contradictory, and have thus recommended respectively the replacement languages of formal logic or poetry as the tools of inquiry. It is the evolution of the conflict within analytic philosophy that occupies the rest of the chapter. The divide that has occurred within linguistic philosophy can be illustrated by considering the work of Quine. On the one hand he brilliantly captures the important points in the philosophy of common sense by showing how ordinary language and beliefs are our inevitable starting-points in inquiry; but on the other he recommends a canonical notation which eliminates many of the idioms commonly used in the humanities and the social sciences, such as talk of intentions. A close look at Quine's philosophy will provide us with a good summary account of the conflicting forces currently at work within the philosophy of common sense.

COMMON SENSE AND QUINE'S CANONICAL NOTATION

The first chapter of *Word and Object* places Quine squarely within the tradition of common sense. He begins, as does Reid, by taking issue with certain simplified empiricist notions, ones found, for example, in Berkeley: talk of sense data is parasitic upon common sense, this being quite simply "ordinary talk of physical things."[36] We learn first of everyday objects, and only later can we conceive the possibility of reduction to sensory stimulations: "Entification begins at arm's length; the points of condensation in the primordial conceptual scheme are things glimpsed, not glimpses";[37] thus "our conceptual firsts are middle-sized, middle-distanced objects."[38] He also takes to be perverse the idea of a more primitive language than ordinary language. When considering the claim that a "protocol language" would be better understood, or be based on better

---

[36] *Word and Object* (Cambridge, Mass.: M.I.T. Press, 1960), p. 3.
[37] Ibid., p. 1.   [38] Ibid., pp. 4–5.

evidence, Quine makes much the same point as Malcolm that such an interpretation of the concepts of "understanding" and "evidence" would involve "depriving them of the very denotations to which they mainly owe such sense as they make to us."[39] Quine's use of the paradigm case argument is also nicely illustrated when he considers skepticism:

> We cannot significantly question the reality of the external world, or deny that there is evidence of external objects in the testimony of our senses; for, to do so is simply to dissociate the terms "reality" and "evidence" from the very applications which originally did most to invest those terms with whatever intelligibility they may have for us.[40]

He therefore argues that "to disavow the very core of common sense . . . is no laudable perfectionism; it is a pompous confusion."[41] Harking back to the opening salvo in the war of common sense on empiricism, Quine claims that "to begin with, at least, we have little better to go on than Johnsonian" understanding of physical objects.[42]

But he soon parts company with both Johnson and ordinary language philosophers, the latter of whom he believes, unfairly perhaps in the case of Wittgenstein, to have made current linguistic practices sacrosanct and to have ignored language's constant evolution. Common sense is not static, it progresses with science, for "science is self-conscious common sense."[43] Although critical of the more primitive versions of empiricism, Quine considers himself an empiricist, although one who repudiates the "dogmas" of sense data reductionism and the analytic/synthetic distinction. As such he sees common sense and its more systematic incarnation, science, as a "tool, ultimately, for predicting future experience in the light of past experience."[44] There is thus, as pointed out in the case of Popper, nothing sacrosanct about the beliefs of common sense; they are retained so long as they remain useful. Common sense limits our starting-points, but not where we

---

[39] Ibid., p. 3.
[40] "The Scope and Language of Science," in *The Ways of Paradox* 2nd edn (Cambridge, Mass.: Harvard, 1976), p. 229.
[41] "The Scope and Language of Science," pp. 229–30.
[42] *Word and Object*, p. 3.
[43] Ibid., p. 3. See also "Two Dogmas of Empiricism", in *From a Logical Point of View* 2nd edn (Cambridge, Mass.: Harvard, 1980), p. 45.
[44] "Two Dogmas", p. 44.

end up. Our ideas of ordinary physical objects, for example, are posits which up to now have proven helpful in organizing our experiences; but as posits they are "comparable, epistemologically, to the gods of Homer."[45] Quine believes physical objects are a more fruitful posit than Homeric gods, and thus it would be a scientific error to prefer otherwise. But the sanctity accorded physical objects by previous common sense philosophers is, he suggests, largely because "the hypothesis of ordinary things is shrouded in pre-history."[46] None the less, this should not cause us to lose sight of the fact that a belief of common sense is an hypothesis, and as such is subject to all the considerations which cause hypotheses to be abandoned. As an example of how Quine's understanding of common sense and its critical evolution could "shock" someone like Moore, and has shocked Strawson, he speculates that we could end up one day with a more powerful set of posits which accords no existence to ordinary physical things. "*Such* eventual departures from Johnsonian usage could partake of the spirit of science and even of the evolutionary spirit of ordinary language itself."[47] Although Quine says in *Word and Object* that he will not follow such a path, he later considered the possibility that a field theory, one that does away with the "primordial posits" of bodies, may be "more to the point," and that "all physical objects go by the board", to be replaced by "a theory in which various states are directly ascribed in varying degrees to various regions of space-time."[48] At one point he even criticizes Nelson Goodman for according reality to the common sense world of "sticks, stones, people, and other coarse objects."[49]

Quine views physical objects, or any of the objects of science, as posits due to his belief in the underdetermination of theory by observation. This view constitutes his fundamental break with earlier forms of empiricism. Both words and sentences are too short a construction to bear the load of observational conditionals; this is

---

[45] Ibid.
[46] *Word and Object*, p. 22.
[47] Ibid., p. 4. The views of Quine and Moore concerning existence are nicely summarized in P. F. Strawson, "Moore and Quine," in *Analysis and Metaphysics* (Oxford University Press, 1992).
[48] "Facts of the Matter," in *Essays on the Philosophy of W. V. Quine*, edited by R. W. Shahan and C. Swoyer (Norman: University of Oklahoma Press, 1979), pp. 164–5.
[49] "Goodman's Ways of Worldmaking," in *Theories and Things* (Cambridge, Mass.: Belknap, 1981), p. 97.

done by theories as a whole. But there is a parallel here between his scientific holism and his theory of radical translation: there is no fact of the matter either in translation or science; there may be competing theories which account for all the same observations both in nature and in verbal behavior. The notion of meaning as some occult entity to which translation is to be faithful is found to be extraneous; explicating the meaning of a phrase is merely the act of translation into other language. The parallel drawn between the theory of nature and the theory of translation now raises the possibility that science faces the same relativism as translation. Quine considers this interpretation: "Have we now so far lowered our sights as to settle for a relativistic doctrine of truth – rating the statements of each theory as true for that theory, and brooking no higher criticism?"[50] Quine escapes this conclusion, as did Popper, by recourse to Tarski's semantic account of truth. Philosophical skepticism has often resulted from a prior belief in truth as correspondence with the way the world is objectively. Tarski pointed out that this schema makes sense only if we have a meta-language in which to talk about a sentence and the state of affairs it describes. Quine makes use of Tarski's account. Taking a meta-language, L, the name of a sentence in the object language, s, and a translation of s in the meta-language, p, we derive a notion of truth relativized to L. Thus:

"Brutus killed Caesar" is true if and only if Brutus killed Caesar.

According to this interpretation, ascription of truth is merely a device for indicating which sentences we are willing to affirm; saying that a sentence is true is to assert the sentence. This is also Ramsey's redundancy theory of truth. Or, in Quine's words, "Ascription of truth just cancels the quotation marks. Truth is disquotation."[51] Even though there is no account of truth that is not relativized to a meta-language, when we assert a sentence we stand by its truth in a non-relativized fashion. As Christopher Hookway makes the point, for a thoroughgoing relativism of the sort considered by Quine to be possible "there must be no sentences that we use rather than mention: yet assertion involves the use of a

---

[50] *Word and Object*, p. 24.
[51] *Pursuit of Truth*, 2nd edn (Cambridge, Mass.: Harvard University Press, 1992), p. 80.

sentence. So total explicit relativism is inconsistent with the making of any assertions at all."[52] This point can used to interpret Quine's claim that "the saving consideration is that we continue to take seriously our own particular aggregate science."[53] According to Hookway, "we take our commonsense beliefs seriously by using them as a basis for action. Our commonsense view of the world provides a background against which we conduct our projects and activities."[54] In other words, in common sense we continually make assertions, and stand by their truth in a non-relativized fashion. If, as Hookway claims, Quine shares with Popper's Commonsense Realism and Peirce's Critical Commonsensism a continuity between theoretical science and common sense, then the sentences of science will share the same committment to truth. Thus, against Descartes, Quine says "we own and use our beliefs of the moment ... [and] we can judge truth as earnestly and absolutely as can be; subject to correction, but that goes without saying."[55] The truth of a statement is not seen as lying in the possession of some abstract property such as correspondence with objective reality; the truth is a result of the concrete reasons presented for claiming it to be true. Davidson draws on essentially the same idea when he claims that it makes no sense to say with the skeptic that we may have no true beliefs at all. Because we cannot imagine an alternative conceptual scheme, the bulk of our common sense beliefs must be true. It is only within our inherited conceptual scheme that doubt is possible. This account of truth constitutes today a powerful defence of the beliefs of common sense, at least as a whole rather than individually. Quine like his predecessors in the tradition has used common sense as a philosophical defense against skepticism.

Quine provides another interpretation of common sense that specifies its role in empirical rather than philosophical questions. This comes out when he discusses choice between theories. Midway between observation and self-evident truths are hypotheses, which Quine approximates as "enlightened guesswork."[56] Hypotheses are valued, *caeteris paribus*, according to several virtues they may possess, these being simplicity, generality, refutability, modesty,

---

[52] "Indeterminacy and Interpretation," in *Action and Interpretation*, edited by C. Hookway and P. Pettit (Cambridge University Press, 1978), p. 29.
[53] *Word and Object*, p. 24.   [54] "Indeterminacy and Interpretation," p.30.
[55] *Word and Object*, pp. 24–5.
[56] *The Web Of Belief* 2nd edn (New York: Random House, 1978), p. 65.

and, most importantly for our purposes, conservatism.[57] One hypothesis is more conservative than another if it conflicts with fewer accepted beliefs. This is valued because in the course of inquiry a conservative step, one that involves abandoning less of what is currently accepted, limits the chances of great error. "The longer the leap . . . the more serious an angular error in the direction. For a leap in the dark the likelihood of a happy landing is severely limited. Conservatism holds out the advantages of limited liability."[58] In other words, in the market for scientific knowledge the assumption of risk-neutrality is unrealistic: we are not indifferent to the variance of theoretical return. Quine suggests that scientists' revealed preferences are risk-averse.[59] This does not mean, of course, that there are no revolutionary steps, merely that the loss of conservatism should be paid for by gains in, say, simplicity. Our understanding of common sense, as the first line of defence against cranks, can now be seen in Quine's hands to be synonymous with the virtue of conservatism. Common sense may indeed be reactionary, but so much the better! That is its job.

A succinct version of this argument is made, ironically, by David Lewis in the course of defending his theory of possible worlds against what he calls "the incredulous stare" argument. He points out other virtues of theories, in particular the economy and simplicity of his own modal realism, but recognizes as well that theory cannot break with too much of what has gone before. "And much of what we thought before was just common sense. Common sense is a settled body of theory – unsystematic folk theory – which at any rate we *do* believe."[60] He shares with Quine, although apart

---

[57] Ibid., ch. 6.   [58] Ibid., pp. 67–8.

[59] Theoretical risk profiles could be different depending on the disciplines; and these preferences in turn could be a function of what is at stake. One would expect the policy sciences to display a greater degree of risk aversion because of the magnitude of the potential damage done by a rash "leap in the dark." In other words, it is not wise to gamble with economic and political theory. This may be another perspective from which to view the claims of, for example, Monetarists, who emphasize our limited ability to understand and fine-tune the economy. Such could also be said of conservative political theorists such as Burke. Alternatively, if the political theorist is speaking for a class with little vested interest in the current system, as was Marx, then his profile would be that of a risk-taker. Of course, Marx willing accepted the political risk inherent in his theory. The epistemic risk is different, more like a second-order risk, the risk that one is wrong. It is not inconceivable for an epistemically risk-averse theorist to arrive at a radical political theory, as was perhaps the case with Gramsci, or a radical economic theory. This was perhaps the case with Keynes, as we will see below.

[60] *On the Plurality of Worlds*, (Oxford: Blackwell, 1986), p. 134.

from this the similarities obviously cease, the following understanding of common sense:

Common sense has no absolute authority in philosophy. It's not that the
folk know in their blood what the highfalutin' philosophers may forget.
And it's not that common sense speaks with the voice of some infallible
faculty of "intuition." It's just that theoretical conservatism is the
only sensible policy for theorists of limited power, who are duly modest
about what they could accomplish after a fresh start. Part of this
conservatism is reluctance to accept theories that fly in the face of
common sense.[61]

In the tradition of critical commonsensism, common sense and
science are not seen in conflict; rather the former is taken to be the
current state of theory. If common sense has a claim to be heard its
claim is nothing more than the counsel of conservatism in the
choice of hypotheses. Listening to common sense is thus, as Quine
says, both a "counsel of laziness and a strategy of discovery."[62] But
as such it is a claim to be balanced against other hypothetical
virtues.

Foremost among the other virtues Quine considers is simplicity.
Our innate ideas of simplicity are "more easily sensed than
described," although Occham's razor embodies the essential
point.[63] Newton's hypothesis of universal gravitation, for example,
was "simpler than its predecessors in that it covered in a brief
unified story what had previously been covered only by two
unrelated accounts" of planetary and terrestrial mechanics.[64] Our
preference for simple theories is partly aesthetic, partly recommended by the obvious fact that simple theories are easier to work
with. The preference is also defended on the same grounds as
conservatism, because it limits liability: "the more complex the
hypothesis, the more and wilder ways of going wrong."[65] There
is one further rationale Quine provides for the operation of
the hypothetical virtues, a rationale distinct from "cagy strategy."[66]
He questions how it is that notions of simplicity can guide us to
true theories about nature, given that these notions are essentially aesthetic. His answer to this charge of relativism is as
follows:

---

[61] Ibid.   [62] *Word and Object*, p. 20.
[63] Ibid., p. 19.   [64] *Web of Belief*, p. 71.
[65] Ibid., p. 72.   [66] Ibid.

Darwin's theory of natural selection offers a causal connection between subjective simplicity and objective truth in the following way. Innate subjective standards of simplicity that make people prefer some hypothesis to others will have survival value insofar as they favor successful prediction. Those who predict best are likeliest to survive and reproduce their kind, in a state of nature anyway, and so their innate standards of simplicity are handed down.[67]

Quine focuses almost exclusively on the two qualities of simplicity and conservatism, implying at times that scientific progress derives its momentum from the innovative impulse to simplify being tempered by the drag of conservatism. However, in considering the role of these two properties in the balancing act that is theoretical choice Quine displays his impatience with common sense: "Whenever simplicity and conservatism are known to counsel opposite courses, the verdict of conscious methodology is on the side of simplicity. Conservatism is nevertheless the preponderant force, but no wonder; it can still operate when stamina and imagination fail."[68] Quine, like Lewis, does indeed tip his hat to common sense, but then quickly moves on to place more weight on the virtue of simplicity. In so doing both end up saying things which would, and do, "shock" philosophers whose preferences tilt more to the counsel of common sense. Quine and Lewis may have recognized a role for common sense; that does not mean they are not willing to trade it off at a low price. Seen in this light the claims of common sense boil down to choices as to how much of common sense to trade off in the pursuit of other features of theory. Lewis, after his insightful words on conservatism, immediately acknowledges "that my denial of common sense opinion is severe."[69] And Quine's interests in the construction of his canonical notation are almost exclusively in the simplification of theory. The contrast with Moore is instructive here. Although one of the fountainheads of analysis, he considered common sense to be a tether on our imaginations and technical skill; for him common sense was primary with analysis in its service. Today the order of priority is often reversed, as it is with Lewis and Quine, with the givens of natural language being traded in in the interests of constructing a fully extensional language.

---

[67] Ibid., p. 73. See as well *Word and Object*, p. 20.
[68] *Word and Object*, pp. 20–1.   [69] *On the Plurality of Worlds*, p. 135.

Quine's commitment to extensionalism in the form of his canonical notation entails a dramatic simplification of the theory of common sense. A large number of the idioms of natural language have to be reformulated so as to leave only the quantification and truth functions of the predicate calculus. This is required because a scientifically adequate language, according to Quine, must eliminate all "sources of truth-value fluctuation,"[70] such as the idioms common in ordinary language which admit referentially opaque contexts, ie. contexts that are non-extensional. Thus the canonical notation cannot admit tense, quotation, vagueness, or the propositional attitudes. Alternatively, the theory cannot be committed ontologically to entities lacking clear identity conditions. Lack of clear individuation is one of Quine's main objections to the notion of possible worlds. With referentially transparent contexts quantification may proceed, and it is here that theory displays its ontological commitments. Russell had shown with his theory of descriptions how an apparently referring definite description in ordinary use may be hiding its true logical form. Similarly, Quine shows that a term with an apparently referential function is not necessarily so unless embedded in the wider context of a truly referring idiom. Names, for example, can be translated into descriptions and descriptions eliminated by means of Russell's theory. The only way we unequivocally commit ourselves to an entity's existence is through the apparatus of quantification, this "being a device for talking in general of objects."[71] Ontic commitment occurs when an entity falls within the range of a bound variable. Hence Quine's enigmatic dictum: "To be assumed as an entity is, purely and simply, to be reckoned as the value of a variable."[72] A theory postulates the existence of only those things required to make the theory true. Quine's canonical notation thus links ontology with a logically ideal language in a manner somewhat similar to that of Wittgenstein's and Russell's logical atomism. "If we are limning the true and ultimate structure of reality, the canonical scheme for us is the austere scheme that knows no quotation but direct quotation and no propositional attitudes but only the physical constitution and behaviour of

[70] *Word and Object*, p. 228.   [71] *Word and Object*, p. 242.
[72] "On What there Is," in *From a Logical Point of View*, p. 13.

organisms."[73] It differs greatly from logical atomism in that the connection between logic and ontology is not the unique and necessary one proposed by Russell and Wittgenstein. Radical translation makes nonsense of this idea. The canonical notation is a translation of ordinary language; it is a theory and as such is without relations of synonymy and is underdetermined by linguistic behavior. Again approaching the suggestion of relativism he says, "Nor let it be retorted that such constructions are conventional affairs not dictated by reality; for may not the same be said of a physical theory? True, such is the nature of reality that one physical theory will get us around better than another; but similarly for canonical notations."[74]

The logical simplification Quine has achieved is matched by an equally minimalist ontology. This comes out clearly in his few comments on psychology and the social sciences, for here he is a thoroughgoing physicalist. By this he means that "nothing happens in the world, not the flutter of an eyelid, not the flicker of a thought, without some redistribution of microphysicial states."[75] Physical events are primary, and mental events cannot take place without some change in the physical state of the person. Physics is thus taken as the basic science, the one that "investigates the essential nature of the world"; other sciences such as biology describe "a local bump" and the human sciences such as psychology describe "a bump on the bump."[76] Quine does not take this view to entail physiological reductionism because "the groupings of events in mentalistic terms need not stand in any systematic relation to biological groupings."[77] This physicalism dovetails, as mentioned, with his views on the sorts of entities that fit into an extensional language. Intentions are one such type of entity that are inadmissable on account of their irreducible vagueness.[78] The impossibility of specifying meaning as an entity to which translation must be adequate entails the "emptiness of a science of intention."[79] And "because the grammar of the belief idiom outruns its factuality, the idiom is not acceptable as an idiom of an austere scientific

---

[73] *Word and Object*, p. 221.   [74] Ibid., p. 161.
[75] "Goodman's Ways of Worldmaking," p. 98.
[76] "Smart's Philosophy and Scientific Realism," in *Theories and Things*, p. 93.
[77] "Facts of the Matter," p. 163.
[78] *Pursuit of Truth*, pp. 65–7, and 71–3.   [79] *Word and Object*, p. 221.

language."[80] Quine sees little to be gained from admitting intentions into this language, the only reason people have thought otherwise being the occurrence in ordinary language of the idiom of belief ascription. This is another case where his canonical notation is to improve on the logically misleading forms of ordinary language. Quine's physicalism and extensionalism is not dogmatic in its revisionary zeal; non-fundamental sciences cannot do without their more convenient languages. Indeed, in his latest writings he goes so far as to suggest that he accepts Davidson's anomalistic monism.[81] But it does make some sort of claim, even without implying the need for reconstruction, that these sciences are not investigating the ultimate properties of the world; they have the lesser task of studying "bumps."

Quine's philosophy successfully accounts for our intuitions concerning common sense: why it should be listened to, and why it is not infallible. He has thus avoided sounding reactionary, as many other common sense philosophers have; common sense is not a timeless faculty of intuition; nor is a recognition of its role in thought tantamount to fossilizing current beliefs. Common sense is the inevitable starting-point for further inquiry. However, many who are critical of Quine's canonical notation and physicalist ontology have implicitly disagreed with the relative weights put on simplicity and conservatism in his ideal language. This is particularly the case with philosophers who have more involvement with the social sciences and humanities.

Rorty, for one, wants to reclaim the intellectual respectability of the humanities and interpretive social sciences. He accepts Quine's view of the "gradual holistic adjustment made famous by 'Two Dogmas of Empiricism'" but questions "Why should not the unit of empirical inquiry be the whole of culture . . . rather than just the whole of physical science?"[82] This is the right question. Quine is at his least convincing when dealing with the intellectual tools required to negotiate the social world. It is telling, for example, that he rarely discusses the ethical dimension of common sense, as did previous common sense philosophers. For Quine, common

---

[80] "Let Me Accentuate the Positive," in *Reading Rorty* edited by A. Malachowski (Oxford: Blackwell, 1990), pp. 117–18. See as well the succinct discussion in "Facts of the Matter," pp. 166–9.
[81] *Pursuit of Truth*, p. 72.
[82] *Philosophy and the Mirror of Nature* (Princeton University Press, 1979), p. 201.

sense is primarily our native theory of the physical world. He does mention the Skinnerian training of our moral responses; and he briefly discusses how altruistic intuitions are accounted for by natural selection, how they contribute to the "continuation of the genetic pool."[83] But the frequent recourse to Darwinian explanation raises a difficulty. Choice of a theory can be defended on the grounds of its relative simplicity; and simplicity in turn is defended by its proven survival value. So it is the contribution to the advancement of our welfare that is the ultimate goal of our theories, rather than the attainment of an aesthetic ideal for its own sake. Now, Quine recognizes that, "efficacy in communication and in prediction . . . is the ultimate duty of language, science, and philosophy . . . Elegance, conceptual economy, also enters as an objective. But this virtue, engaging though it is, is secondary."[84] But if survival, both theoretical and physical, is the criterion, it seems unjustified to claim that modern physics alone can be defended along these lines. Modern political theory, admittedly with some major disasters, has been of primary importance to the advancement of our welfare. One could argue that a persuasive and shared account of civil society is a prerequisite for natural science to perform the task assigned it by Quine. Perhaps the same could be said of the visual arts and literature. But these are worlds, or versions of worlds, that Quine does not admit into his ontology.[85] He may recognize the utility of the languages used in more cultural fields, but again sees "factuality threatened . . . by vagueness and dimness of criteria."[86] The idioms used here are thus not admissable in his canonical notation. However, in thinking that such translatability is the hallmark of science Quine is putting simplicity before utility. There are two possible interpretations to put on his argument. If he believes that the translation is required before, say, a social science becomes truly scientific, which by another of his criterion means contributing to communication and prediction, then I believe the rejoinder is that he has done too little research in social theory to know which idioms are useful; his dictum becomes nothing more than a methodological prescription

---

[83] *Web of Belief*, pp. 136–8. See as well, "On the Nature of Moral Values," in *Theories and Things*, pp. 55–66.
[84] "Identity, Ostension, and Hypothesis," *From a Logical Point of View*, p. 79.
[85] He considers these worlds in "Goodman's Ways of Worldmaking," pp. 97–8.
[86] "Let Me Accentuate the Positive," p. 118.

of the most dubious kind. The question of which idiom or language is most useful for a social science is one that only experienced social scientists can answer. If, on the other hand, his attitude is that we should continue using the looser idioms of the humanities if these have proven useful, but none the less refuse to recognize their onto-logical claims, then the natural response is: so what? Ontological access becomes a worthless prize. Both of these interpretations can be found in Quine's few comments on the subject. They are connected by the assumption that only entities entering into quantification have clear identity conditions. But neither argument successfully leads to his prescriptive dictums on the nature of scientific discourse. The ontological argument for his canonical notation turns out to be quite vacuous; and without it we are left with his pragmatic argument for the utility of an idiom. In his own words, "efficacy in communication and in prediction . . . is the ultimate duty of language, science, and philosophy." When discussing the appropriate languages for the social sciences, we should, then, take a candid look at which idioms promote them, rather than approach them with a sole concern for logical simplification.

In anticipation of a later chapter it is worth at this point men-tioning that Keynes, during the ascendancy of logical atomism, was skeptical of the purported connection between an ontology and a logical notation:

This question, which faces all contemporary writers on logical and philosophical subjects, is in my opinion much more a question of *style* – and therefore to be settled on the same sort of considerations as other such questions – than is generally supposed.[87]

Keynes recognized that the question of an appropriate language is more a question of communication, to be judged by criteria appropriate to that question. I turn to his discussion of these criteria later. In the next chapter we turn back in time to take a closer look at how the debate we have been following between linguistic revisionists and conservatives was played out in Cambridge philosophy during the thirties. There too we find a case made for an ideal language, and opposed to this reductionism a case for the unanalysability and serviceability of ordinary language.

---

[87] *Collected Works*, vol. 8, p. 20.

Wittgenstein, Ramsey, Keynes, and, to a lesser extent, Moore examined the role of simplicity and common sense in formulating our beliefs. Wittgenstein concluded that the vagueness of ordinary language is not an impediment to communication but can be a virtue in language. Keynes then applied his analysis of vague concepts to the social sciences and similarly concluded that they play an indispensable role in handling complex social phenomena. His argument did not merely consist in placing greater weight on the virtue of conservatism in social theory; he also questioned whether formalization did in fact lead to a simplification of theory. Simplification, both Keynes and Wittgenstein found, is served by vague concepts.

CHAPTER 2

Ideal languages and vague concepts: the transition in Cambridge philosophy

In the next few chapters I sketch out how the conflicting demands of common sense and a canonical notation played themselves out in Cambridge philosophy between the Wars. The focus is on Moore, Wittgenstein, and Keynes, although in later chapters Ramsey and Sraffa are also brought in to the discussion. The account of the transition in Cambridge philosophy of necessity must be highly selective, and it will deal exclusively with the idea of an ideal language in early logical atomism, and on how Wittgenstein's later rediscovery of the property of vagueness challenged this notion. Much of later Cambridge philosophy chose the opposite route to that taken by Quine in balancing the demands of a canonical notation with those of common sense, and Keynes in particular indicated a position which nicely focuses the debate on whether vague concepts simplify or complicate theoretical activity.

AN IDEAL LANGUAGE

There were various schools of analysis but they all shared the practice of rewriting philosophically puzzling statements in more precise language. Wittgenstein pointed out that the origin of this method lay in the fascination with a single form of explanation: the common practice of substituting one expression for another in order to clear up a misunderstanding was taken as a paradigm case of problem solving; and "this," he wrote, "may be called an 'analysis' of our forms of expression, for the process is sometimes like one of taking a thing apart."[1] Russell had displayed the usefulness of this practice when dealing with the contradiction involved in discussing non-existent entities such as the present King of France:

---

[1] *Investigations*, sect. 90.

it was thought that these entities must possess some sort of ontological status if we can understand the terms referring to them, but it was not understood what form of being non-existent entities could possess without invoking "some shadowy Platonic world of being."[2] The theory of descriptions presented a way of reformulating such statements in a manner that did not impute being to non-existent entities: a proposition of the sort "The present King of France is bald" could be translated into "There is one and only one thing which is the King of France and it is bald." It is now evident that the statement is claiming the existence of a king of France and is therefore false. The reformulation has avoided the implication that the non-existent king has some sort of being.

The success of Russell's theory inspired the analytic philosophers towards the goal of making explicit the true logical structure of language. If this were done then we would see that most philosophical problems arise because the structure is misunderstood. In the *Tractatus* Wittgenstein claimed that "Most of the propositions and questions of philosophers arise from our failure to understand the logic of our language."[3] And he recognized that "It was Russell who performed the service of showing that the apparent logical form of a proposition need not be its real one."[4] This view of philosophy and language has a clearly revisionary bias, as it implies that our language can, and should, be made to display its sense precisely:

The idea is to express in an appropriate symbolism what in ordinary language leads to endless misunderstandings. That is to say, where ordinary language disguises logical structure, where it allows the formation of pseudopropositions, where it uses one term in an infinity of different meanings, we must replace it by a symbolism which gives a clear picture of the logical structure, excludes pseudopropositions, and uses its terms unambiguously.[5]

Two different types of analysis were proposed for displaying the logical form lying beneath the surface of thought, and these two

---

[2] Bertrand Russell, *My Philosophical Development* (London: Unwin, 1959), p. 64.
[3] *Tractatus Logico-Philosophicus*, translated by D. F. Pears and B. F. McGuinness (London: Routledge & Kegan Paul, 1961), 4.003.
[4] *Tractatus*, 4.0031.
[5] "Some Remarks on Logical Form," *Proceedings of the Aristotelian Society*, supp. vol. 9 (1929), p. 163.

possibilities set up a tension within Cambridge philosophy. Logical, or same-level, analysis, exposed the logical structure hidden in a statement by rewording it, as was done with the sentence concerning the King of France; new-level, reductive, or philosophical analysis, as it was variously called, aimed at reducing all terms to the basic facts of experience; it involved, in Russell's words "getting down to the ultimate simples, out of which the world is built, simples having a kind of reality not belonging to anything else."[6] Thus in new-level analysis entities under examination might be resolved further into sense-data or atoms out of which they are comprised. In advancing this theory, known as logical atomism, the early analytic philosophers displayed their kinship with many previous philosophical systems by attempting to anchor knowledge in unanalyzable intuitions. For Russell and Wittgenstein of the *Tractatus* the postulated fundamental units of analysis were logical atoms, and they thought that any meaningful proposition was a truth-functional compound of atomic propositions. The "propositional calculus" was, as Russell termed it, a "logically perfect language," an "ideal language."[7]

Russell and Wittgenstein, however, differed greatly over the interpretation given to this ideal language. Russell took it to represent a goal to which we aim in reformulating language: "the whole function of language is to have meaning, and it only fulfills this function in proportion as it approaches to the ideal language that we postulate."[8] Wittgenstein, on the other hand, had claimed that "all the propositions of our everyday language, just as they stand, are in perfect logical order."[9] So while Russell conceived of the ideal as something to be emulated, Wittgenstein interpreted his own efforts as laying bare a structure that was already present, albeit disguised, in ordinary language. His goal was to identify the inherent logic in order to show that philosophical problems arose through it being misunderstood. In P. M. S. Hacker's words:

Certainly we want a perfect conceptual notation for philosophical purposes, and the *Tractatus* is intended to provide the fundamental principles for such a notation. But . . . this is not in order to put into

---

[6] Quoted in J. O. Urmson, *Philosophical Analysis. Its Development Between the Two World Wars* (Oxford: Clarendon, 1956), p. 40. See as well *Tractatus*, 2.0201.
[7] Introduction to *Tractatus*, p. x.
[8] Ibid.   [9] *Tractatus*, 5.5563.

language something which is not yet there, but to reveal the underlying logical structure of language.[10]

Looking back at this ideal, Wittgenstein indicated how Russell's form of same-level analysis, which was designed as a tool for the resolution of philosophical problems, suggested the more revisionary project of new-level analysis. He confessed that his own ideas "may make it look as if we saw it as our task to reform language."[11] Explaining the drift of early analytic philosophy he wrote:

But now it may come to look as if there were something like a final analysis of our forms of language, and so a *single* completely resolved form of every expression. That is, as if our usual forms of expression were, essentially, unanalysed; as if there were something hidden in them that had to be brought to light. When this is done the expression is completely clarified and our problem solved.

It can also be put like this: we eliminate misunderstandings by making our expressions more exact; but now it may look as if we were moving towards a particular state, a state of complete exactness; and as if this were the real goal of our investigation.[12]

Moore's influence on the Cambridge philosophers tempered the revisionary bias inherent in this line of philosophy, for he success-fully convinced most of his colleagues that the task of analysis was not to question the givens of common sense, but, if possible, to vindicate them. As Urmson puts it, Moore's defense of common sense "confirmed the analysts in their view that their job was to analyse, not to question, the deliveries of science and of common sense, for Moore had a devastating way with those who denied his common sense knowledge."[13] Keynes, in his essay "My Early Beliefs," also mentioned Moore's overwhelming influence on the students and philosophers in Cambridge at that time, and in a partly humorous, but also telling, passage recorded Moore's method of argumentation:

Moore at this time was a master of this method – greeting one's remarks with a gasp of incredulity – *Do* you *really* think *that*, an expression of face as if to hear such a thing said reduced him to a state of wonder verging on

---

[10] *Insight and Illusion: Wittgenstein on Philosophy and the Metaphysics of Experience* (Oxford University Press, 1972), p. 15.
[11] *Investigations*, sect. 132.
[12] Ibid., sect. 91.   [13] *Philosophical Analysis*, p. 49.

imbecility, with his mouth wide open and wagging his head in the negative so violent that his hair shook. *Oh!* he would say, goggling at you as if either you or he must be mad; and no reply was possible.[14]

While the analysts who practiced the new-level method thought that the givens of common sense had to be proved through reductive analyses, or at any rate, reformulated in a manner which displayed their truth, Moore accepted a proposition such as "The world has existed for many years past" as true as "it would ordinarily be understood";[15] and he believed that with most propositions of this sort we are unable to give a precise analysis of their meaning. It is ironic that Moore pioneered the very methods of analysis and reduction to sense data later used to question the givens of common sense. Needless to say his attitude to these ideas was much more ambivalent than that of, say, Russell. But suffice it for the moment to say that he did not give reductive analyses any priority over the propositions of common sense: he wrote, "of the *truth* of these propositions there seems to me to be no doubt, but as to what is the correct analysis of them there seems to me to be the gravest doubt."[16] He concluded his defense of common sense by pointing out that others, employing his ideas on analysis, have drawn diametrically opposite conclusions:

Many philosophers, on the other hand, seem to me to have assumed that there is little or no doubt as to the correct analysis of such propositions; and many of these, just reversing my position, have also held that the propositions themselves are not true.[17]

Wittgenstein had earlier sided with the analytics, but he began to express doubts that bore at least a family resemblance to those of Moore. Specifically, he questioned how it was that the logical structure of the *Tractatus* was implicit in, or was prior to, or imparted meaning to, everyday language. He was concerned with defending the forms of everyday language, while Moore, on the other hand, defended certain common sense beliefs. But they did share the belief that the analytic reconstruction of the logic of our language was misconceived. Wittgenstein's move away from the

---

[14] *Collected Works*, vol. 10, p. 438.
[15] G. E. Moore, "A Defence of Common Sense," in *Contemporary British Philosophy*, 2nd series, edited by J. H. Muirhead (Cambridge University Press, 1903), p. 197.
[16] Ibid., p. 223.   [17] Ibid.

earlier reductionist approach, however, followed its own route, one that caused him to become critical of Moore's method.

Wittgenstein's own defense of ordinary language involved taking issue with the theory of meaning he and Russell had accepted at the time of the *Tractatus*. This was a theory informed by several traditional philosophical preconceptions. Russell and Wittgenstein accepted Frege's assumption that concepts had to be precise for only then could we lay down exact rules for their use. They added to this the view that only a determinate referent can impart meaning to a word, and that determinate referents cannot be composite entities, but only the simple, basic constituents of the world – the atoms of logical atomism. Wittgenstein discovered several problems with his form of linguistic atomism. The most obvious one was, as Friedrich Waismann recorded, "the fact that no one has ever succeeded in producing a single atomic proposition."[18] Wittgenstein in fact never proposed any candidates for his simple objects; he deduced their necessity from his theory of meaning. Several of his followers at the time, the philosophers of the Vienna Circle in particular, made a more concerted effort at specifying atomic facts. Stephen Toulmin and Alan Janik explain how this notion lived on in the work of the logical positivists:

Wittgenstein had said nothing to indicate how one was to recognize "atomic facts" or "unit propositions" in practice; this had not been his purpose. The logical positivists now remedied this omission. Taking a hint from Mach and from Russell's doctrine of "knowledge-by-acquaintance," they equated Wittgenstein's 'atomic facts' with the indubitable, directly known "hard data" of Mach's and Russell's epistemologies.[19]

Their attempt was a good example of new-level analysis, with sense data being the ultimate simples, "the ultimate carriers of knowledge, each of them recording one single item of sensory evidence, vouchsafed by one single sensation."[20] Wittgenstein, however, remained agnostic on the issue. Norman Malcolm later asked him about these entities and Wittgenstein replied "that it was not his business, as a logician, to try to decide whether this thing or that was a simple thing or a complex thing, that being a purely *empirical*

---

[18] "Language Strata," in *Logic and Language*, 2nd series, edited by Anthony Flew (Basil Blackwell, 1953), p. 28.
[19] *Wittgenstein's Vienna* (New York: Simon and Schuster, 1973), p. 213.
[20] Ibid.

matter!"[21] Malcolm adds "It was clear that he regarded his former opinion as absurd."[22]

Early in his transitional phase Wittgenstein concluded that it makes no sense to speak of absolutely simple objects, as simplicity and complexity are relative to the types of questions being asked of an object: "We use the word 'composite' (and therefore the word 'simple') in an enormous number of different and differently related ways."[23] Wittgenstein also had doubts about the Tractarian account of reference, for it was no longer clear to him how an object external to a word could impart meaning. To illustrate his point with an example from the language of color, the image of red cannot be the thing that imparts meaning to "red" for we do not in fact need to think of the image when using the word anymore than we need to think of walking when walking. Further, no such image could teach us to use the word for we still have to identify the image. Indeed, if we need the image of red to understand the word why not use an actual patch of the colour which is so much more vivid.[24] The point Wittgenstein made here is similar to Aristotle's "Third Man" argument against Plato's theory of forms: by specifying an entity external to a word that bears its meaning one is on the road of infinite regress, for one can always ask in turn what gives the form its meaning. As Wittgenstein said "you have only replaced one set of symbols by another."[25]

Having repudiated the *a priori* demand for referents in the theory of meaning, Wittgenstein also went on to question Frege's demand for precisely defined concepts. In studying language learning and actual language use he discovered that words do not have a unitary meaning. He illustrated this with the example of the word "game":

Consider for example the proceedings that we call "games." I mean board-games, card-games, ball-games, Olympic games, and so on. What is common to them all? – Don't say: "There *must* be something common, or they would not be called 'games'" – but *look and see* whether there is anything common to all. – For if you look at them you will not see something that is common to all, but similarities, relationships, and a whole series of them at that.[26]

21 Norman Malcolm, *Ludwig Wittgenstein: A Memoir* (London: Oxford University Press, 1958), p. 86.
22 Ibid.   23 *Investigations*, sect. 47. Sects. 46–8 discuss the notion of simples.
24 The *Blue and Brown Books* (Oxford: Basil Blackwell, 1958), p. 4.
25 *Blue and Brown Books*, p. 36.   26 *Investigations*, sect. 66.

Here, as in other examinations, he found "a complicated network of similarities overlapping and criss-crossing,"[27] so he suggested that we think of a word's use as a series of language games, each of which bears a "family resemblance"[28] to the others, enabling them all to be understood as the same concept, but at the same time having no one common feature. His "cluster theory" of meaning constituted a break from the earlier assumption of univocity. He traced this assumption to our "tendency to look for something in common to all entities which we commonly subsume under a general term."[29] He began his transitional *Blue and Brown Books* by pointing out that "We are up against one of the great sources of philosophical bewilderment: a substantive makes us look for a thing that corresponds to it."[30] He argued that this assumption is one that

has shackled philosophical investigation; for it has not only led to no result, but also made the philosopher dismiss as irrelevant the concrete cases, which alone could have helped him to understand the usage of the general term.[31]

He related this view to "other primitive, too simple, ideas of the structure of language,"[32] and said it is comparable to thinking that properties of concepts are similar to ingredients: "eg. that beauty is an ingredient of all beautiful things as alcohol is of beer and wine," making it conceivable to separate the beauty from that which is beautiful.[33] However, our knowledge of a concept is not displayed by specifying a defining essence, it is shown in our ability to use the word.

A corollary of this view is Wittgenstein's later belief that understanding a word is not a mental process; it is an ability, and an ability to do something is not necessarily the sort of thing that can be exhaustively communicated, just as we can play tennis without being able to say how we do it. When we learn words we learn them example by example until we can carry on without correction from our teachers, and can even go on to innovate new uses. The unsettling upshot of this is that while we can all use the words in our natural language we find ourselves strangely unable to specify their

---

[27] Ibid.
[28] Ibid., sect. 67.   [29] *Blue and Brown Books*, p. 17.
[30] Ibid., p. 1.   [31] Ibid., pp. 19–20.
[32] Ibid., p. 17.   [33] Ibid.

exact and exhaustive meaning, just as we might know the sound of a clarinet without being able to describe it.[34] This is quite similar to Moore's point that often we are unable to account for the truth of certain common sense propositions even though they attain for us a certainty unparalleled by any philosophical proposition: "We are all, I think, in this strange position that we do *know* many things . . . and yet we do not know how we *know* them."[35] Wittgenstein, addressing the belief that words are used according to strict rules, said:

not only do we not think of the rules of usage – of definitions, etc. – while using language, but when we are asked to give such rules, in most cases we aren't able to do so. We are unable clearly to circumscribe the concepts we use; not because we don't know their real definition, but because there is no real "definition" to them. To suppose that there *must* be would be like supposing that whenever children play with a ball they play a game according to strict rules.[36]

Our words are like blurred pictures, a series of interconnected uses, all with something quite ambiguous and ineffable holding them together; there is an inevitable vagueness attending them. Waismann was influenced by Wittgenstein and similarly concluded that our everyday concepts are like "shapes in a mist."[37] He drew on an apposite quote by Paul Valery in making this point:

You must . . . have noticed this curious fact – that a given word, which may be perfectly obvious when used in the ordinary course of communication, which presents no difficulties whatever when caught up in the give and take of normal conversation, has a way of becoming almost magically embarrassing, strangely resistant and quite unmanageable in definition, as soon as you withdraw it from circulation with the object of examining it closely and apart from its neighbours, as soon, that is, as you try to establish its meaning in isolation from its momentary function.[38]

Waismann pointed out that our everyday words can have a multiplicity of uses, so that "the meanings interpenetrate, and unite into a larger whole, a sort of cloud";[39] he said of these meanings "that they *dissolve into vagueness*."[40]

---

[34] *Investigations*, sect. 78.
[35] "A Defense of Common Sense," p. 206.   [36] *Blue and Brown Books*, p. 25.
[37] "Language Strata," p. 16.   [38] Ibid., p. 15.
[39] Ibid., p. 14.   [40] Ibid.

VAGUENESS

Several of the classic treatments of vagueness date back to this era. Russell, in his introduction to the *Tractatus*, had discussed how vagueness was an impediment to the construction of an ideal language, and, in 1923, wrote an important article on the issue.[41] The later work of Wittgenstein made it of more pressing concern. But it was Max Black's first article on the subject in 1937 which more or less set the terms of the debate.[42] Each of these philosophers, however, had a slightly different definition of the concept, so these should be spelled out. Furthermore, the concept should be distinguished from several neighbouring ones which are often mistaken as synonyms.

Black's definition of vagueness is now the starting-point for most discussions: "A symbol's vagueness is held to consist in the existence of objects concerning which it is intrinsically impossible to say either that the symbol in question does, or does not, apply."[43] The term "bald," for example, is vague: while it is possible to state decisively that the term applies to someone who is hairless and does not to someone with a full head of hair, it is impossible to say exactly when a rapidly receding hairline turns into baldness. The same problem occurs with other words which measure properties along a scale, such as big–small, hot–cold. In all these cases there is a fringe or penumbra of objects, borderline cases, over which decisive judgment is impossible. Crispin Wright has termed predicates lacking sharp boundaries "tolerant" because their application is insensitive to small changes.[44] Moreover, tolerance is not due to laziness on the part of the speaker, nor to the lack of information about the objects; no new evidence would clear up the matter. As Quine puts it, "Where to draw the line between heaps and nonheaps, . . . or between the bald and the thatched, is not determined by the distribution of microphysical states, known or unknown; it remains an open option."[45] The problem also exists for singular terms. Black imagined a museum lined with chairs, objects

---

[41] "Vagueness," *Australasian Journal of Psychology and Philosophy* 1 (1923), 84–92.
[42] "Vagueness: An Exercise in Logical Analysis," *Philosophy of Science* 4 (1937), pp. 427–55. Reprinted in his *Language and Philosophy* (Ithaca: Cornell University Press, 1949).
[43] "Vagueness: An Exercise in Logical Analysis," in *Language and Philosophy*, p. 28.
[44] "On the Coherence of Vague Predicates," p. 333.
[45] "What Price Bivalence," in *Theories and Things*, p. 35.

running from a Chippendale, which is universally recognized as a chair, down to a lump of wood, which is not. In between there are intermediate objects where "personal uncertainty is a reflection of objective lack of agreement."[46] Similarly, it is not clear where a mountain begins, and when there are two mountains rather than one with two peaks. The attendant difficulties are rife, for the property is pervasive. Russell had made this point. He defined a representation as *"vague* when the relation of the representing system to the represented system is not one–one, but one–many."[47] He likened this situation to a smudged picture which could equally be of several people. Since this is characteristic of all representative systems, he concluded: "The fact that meaning is a one–many relation is the precise statement of the fact that all language is more or less vague."[48]

Black thought that Russell's definition involved a confusion between vagueness and generality, so these should be distinguished. Generality "is constituted by the application of a symbol to a multiplicity of objects in the field of reference."[49] It is difficult to find an example that clearly illustrates the difference between this property and vagueness, since most substantives will display both. The term "chair" is general because it applies to a wide range of objects differing in size and shape. Its vagueness refers only to the possibility of finding cases to which it is undecidable whether it applies or not. One could imagine a general term that is not vague, although again examples are hard to find. Alexander Rosenberg proposes "polyhedron" as a concept that is general in its scope without being vague.[50] He does, however, recognize that its definition in terms of solids leaves it open to any vagueness attending this term. Vagueness should also be distinguished from ambiguity, which stems from the existence of several distinct meanings attaching to one word. Ambiguity may be eliminated by distinguishing between these meanings, or by paraphrase.[51] Vagueness should also be distinguished from a property Waismann has termed the 'open

---

[46] "Vagueness: An Exercise in Logical Analysis," p. 33.
[47] "Vagueness," p. 89.   [48] Ibid. p. 90.
[49] "Vagueness: An Exercise in Logical Analysis," p. 29.
[50] "The Virtues of Vagueness in the Languages of Science", *Dialogue* 14 (1975), p. 282.
[51] Quine discusses methods for eliminating ambiguity in *Word and Object*, pp. 129–34. Irving Copilowish has argued that vagueness is a species of ambiguity. "Border-Line Cases, Vagueness, and Ambiguity," *Philosophy of Science* 6 (1939), pp. 192–5.

texture' of a concept. By this he meant that it is impossible in
principle to specify rules that determine the application of an
empirical concept in all circumstances. We devise rules adequate
for cases we know, but we can always imagine new circumstances
where these rules are insufficient for the task of judging whether
the concept is applicable. Vagueness refers to the undecidability of
application of a concept to known cases; open texture points to the
potential failure of definition to prescribe usage in new situations.
As such it is "something like *possibility of vagueness.*"[52]

Lastly, vagueness as a term of interest in semantics should be
distinguished from the meaning of the term when used as one of
reproach. In this mundane sense it refers to slackness of thought or
weakness of prose. Politicians' promises are vague in this sense. The
failure to draw this distinction has led to some misunderstandings
of Wittgenstein. Waismann, for one, can be interpreted as claiming
that all language is vague, while Wittgenstein, while making
ostensively the same point, was pressing the narrower one that no
language could be precise in the manner envisioned by Frege.
Wittgenstein's use of the word is relative to this standard, for
without such a reference it is meaningless to say that language is
either exact or vague. In the *Blue and Brown Books* he cautioned
against using "vagueness" "in a typically metaphysical way, namely
without an antithesis."[53] Similarly, Russell had earlier pointed out:
"We are able to conceive precision; indeed, if we could not do so,
we could not conceive vagueness, which is merely the contrary
of precision."[54] O. K. Bouwsma records that in conversation
Wittgenstein had said: "But neither will it do to suggest as
Waismann seems to, that this language is vague. For there is here
no contrast with some other language which is clear."[55]
Distinguishing between the two interpretations enables us to avoid
the conclusion that Wittgenstein was glorifying defective discourse,
which he was not. Norman Malcolm, echoing Wittgenstein's
concern, wrote:

---

[52] "Verifiability", in *Logic and Language* 1st series, edited by Anthony Flew (Oxford: Basil Blackwell, 1951), p. 120.

[53] p. 46.   [54] "Vagueness," p. 89.

[55] *Wittgenstein: Conversations, 1949–1951*, edited with an introduction by J. L. Craft and Ronald E. Hustwit (Indianapolis: Hackett, 1986), p. 57. However, Wittgenstein then corrects himself by saying "I hadn't better attribute this to Waismann." G. P. Baker and P. M. S. Hacker, on the other hand, do attribute this view to Waismann. *Essays on the*

I refer to his conception that words are not used with "fixed" meanings . . . that concepts do not have "sharp boundaries" . . . This teaching, I believe, produced a tendency in his students to assume that precision and thoroughness were not required in their own thinking.[56]

Wittgenstein was not vindicating sloppy thought or expression. He drew philosophers' attention to the point that precision is relative to the purpose at hand, that there is no absolute standard of precise speech. Language that is vague according to the Fregean definition can be precise according to more practical considerations. Crispin Wright puts the point nicely:

Lack of sharp boundaries is not the reflection of an omission; it is a product of the kind of task to which an expression is put, the kind of consequences which we attach to its application or, more deeply, the continuity of a world which we wish to describe in purely observational terms.[57]

Wittgenstein focused on a type of vagueness that is analytically different from those discussed by Russell and Black. This type of vagueness is entailed by his cluster theory of meaning: there are a number of independently sufficient conditions for the application of words, not just one, a common property shared by the objects subsumed. This makes definition difficult. He recognized that definitions can be given; and misunderstandings can be cleared up by legislating the boundaries of words. But these definitions cannot circumscribe all that we normally consider, say, a game, or a number:

I *can* give the concept "number" rigid limits in this way, that is, use the word "number" for a rigidly limited concept, but I can also use it so that the extension of the concept is *not* closed by a frontier. And this is how we do use the word "game." For how is the concept of a game bounded? What still counts as a game and what no longer does? Can you give the boundary? No. You can *draw* one; for none has so far been drawn. (But that never troubled you before when you used the word "game.")[58]

William Alston has analyzed the type of vagueness implied by the cluster theory of meaning. He distinguishes vagueness stemming

---

Philosophical Investigations. Volume 1. Wittgenstein: Meaning and Understanding (Oxford: Basil Blackwell, 1983), p. 225.
[56] *Memoir*, p. 63.
[57] "On the Coherence of Vague Predicates," p. 330.   [58] *Investigations*, sect. 68.

from the absence of a cut-off point along a scale, as is found with size and age, from vagueness which is caused by a term's having "a number of independent conditions of application."[59] He calls these "degree" and "combination of conditions vagueness" respectively.[60] Russell and Black focused on degree vagueness, while Wittgenstein's cluster theory of meaning emphasized combinatory vagueness. In the example of games, we find not a single defining feature, but several – they involve competition, skill, are played for amusement, etc. Wittgenstein's theory has received two different interpretations. Renford Bambrough considers five objects classified by five properties, ABCDE, and takes Wittgenstein's notion of family resemblance to mean that each of the five objects need have only four of the properties, but lack a fifth, a different one for each object, and still be referred to by the same term.

e	d	c	b	a
ABCD	ABCE	ABDE	ACDE	BCDE

Here there is no common feature but the objects may all be referred to by the same word.[61] Hjalmar Wennerberg points out that according to this interpretation there is no common property, but that any two objects in the series will always share several features. He, on the other hand, thinks that Wittgenstein's account of family resemblance also includes cases where no features are shared, yet the two objects are considered samples of the same concept.[62] Wennerberg illustrates this possibility with the series.

e	d	c	b	a
ABCD	BCDE	CDEF	DEFG	EFGH

Here objects e and a have nothing in common. The family resemblance holding a series together acts locally, like links in a chain, and not globally by means of a common unifying property. On either interpretation understanding the nature of definition is

---

[59] *Dimensions of Meaning* (Englewood Cliffs: Prentice Hall, 1964), p. 87.
[60] Ibid.
[61] "Universals and Family Resemblances," *Proceedings of the Aristotelian Society*, New Series 61 (1960–1), pp. 207–22.
[62] "The Concept of Family Resemblance in Wittgenstein's Later Philosophy," *Theoria* 33 (1967), pp. 107–32.

difficult. It cannot be done by generalizing common properties; it is rather the practice of choosing a sample object to stand as a paradigm case, choosing, that is, what the cognitive psychologist, Eleanor Rosch, and after her the theorists of fuzzy logic have called prototypes. But such a definition will inevitably render a word vague because we cannot say definitely which properties, or how many, are required for a word to apply to an object. Keynes made much of the distinction between identifying a common property to objects, i.e. the process of generalization, and proposing a sample from a diverse population of objects, and he came to think it was, as we will see, important to understanding the nature of definitions and models in the social sciences.

Wittgenstein next considered the Fregean claim that such vague concepts must be flawed. He pointed out that we may not be able to draw an exact boundary around our words in the way Frege had thought necessary, but we can still use them:

If I tell someone "Stand roughly here" – may not this explanation work perfectly? . . . But isn't it an inexact explanation? – Yes; why shouldn't we call it "inexact"? Only let us understand what 'inexact' means. For it does not mean "unusable."[63]

Furthermore, the vagueness may contribute to efficiency of communication:

One might say that the concept "game" is a concept with blurred edges.– "But is a blurred concept a concept at all?" – Is an indistinct photograph a picture of a person at all? Is it even always an advantage to replace an indistinct picture by a sharp one? Isn't the indistinct one often exactly what we need?[64]

This view of language contrasts to that of the *Tractatus*, where language was assumed to operate like "a calculus proceeding according to exact rules,"[65] and in contrast to the ideal language of Russell, who claimed to have "invented a special language with a view to avoiding vagueness."[66] Looking back at his early beliefs, Wittgenstein wrote "we want to say that there can't be any vagueness in logic,"[67] but now concluded that "there must be perfect order even in the vaguest sentence."[68]

---

[63] *Investigations*, sect. 88.   [64] Ibid., sect. 71.

[65] *Blue and Brown Books*, p. 25   [66] "Vagueness," p. 84.

[67] *Investigations*, sect. 101.   [68] Ibid., sect. 98.

Wittgenstein had said in the *Tractatus* that ordinary language was already in order, but he there based this view on the argument that the order was due to his ideal logical structure being implicit in natural language. In the *Investigations* no such argument is made: there is no implicit logical structure, one free of vagueness; there is only the indefinite number of surface 'grammars', and these are now seen to be in perfect logical order as is, with all their attendant vagueness. This contrasts as well with the views of Russell, who wrote that philosophical analysis "is just like . . . watching an object approaching through a thick fog" until we can make out the clear "articulations" of the object. He claimed that "Belief in the above process is my strongest and most unshakable prejudice as regards the methods of philosophical analysis." On the other hand "It seems to me that those who object to analysis would wish us to be content with the initial dark blur."[69]

Wittgenstein did not stop with repudiating the ideal order supposedly lying implicit in everyday language, he went on to question the potential utility of such an ideal language. To begin with, demanding exactness from as simple a command as 'Stand roughly there' is a touch pedantic: we can always demand more precision, "But has this exactness still got a function here: isn't the engine idling?"[70] And what if we could effect a complete analysis? Would this contribute to easing communication? A broom, for example, might in the first instance be analyzed into broomstick and brush:

Then does someone who says that the broom is in the corner really mean: the broomstick is there, and so is the brush? . . . Suppose that instead of saying "Bring me the broom," you said, "Bring me the broomstick and the brush which is fitted on to it"! – Isn't the answer: "Do you want the broom? Why do you put it so oddly?" – Is he going to understand the further analyzed sentence better? – This sentence, one might say, achieves the same as the ordinary one, but in a more roundabout way.[71]

---

[69] *My Philosophical Development*, p. 99. He continued, "The later Wittgenstein . . . seems to have grown tired of serious thinking and to have invented a doctrine which would make such an activity unnecessary" (p. 161). Elsewhere Russell likened ordinary language philosophy to certain anti-intellectual Inquisitions, such as the Abecedarian heresy, which "forsook all study of Holy Scripture and looked for Divine truth at the mouths of those who, by all ordinary men, were accounted the most ignorant of mankind." Foreword to Ernest Gellner, *Words and Things: A Critical Account of Linguistic Philosophy, And a Study in Ideology* (London: Victor Gollancz, 1959), pp. 14–15.
[70] *Investigations*, sect. 88.   [71] Ibid., sect. 60.

Observations such as this led Wittgenstein to conclude that formal logic "is greatly handicapped in comparison with our actual language."[72] Not only was he repudiating the possibility and the necessity of reductive analysis, he was also effecting an inversion of our notions of efficient discourse. Once meaning is located within language games, and is found to be relative to the purpose of each linguistic activity, then the notion of a primary, essentially descriptive, propositional structure is no longer seen as the only one that facilitates communication; and the ideal language of the *Tractatus* can be seen rather as a particularly cumbersome form of discourse compared to everyday language, which is ideally suited for its uses. This leads to an apparently paradoxical conclusion: words in our natural language are inherently vague, and since this means that more goes into a word than can be made explicit in a definition, one is led to the conclusion that there is a precision in vagueness. Strictly circumscribed concepts, at least when dealing with problems formulated in natural language, will leave too much out of account, or will be too cumbersome to achieve their goal of facilitating understanding; our vague concepts, on the other hand, are implicitly understood by native speakers. The more precise statement, by analytic standards, if it did not confuse with its foreign terminology, might achieve the same as an ordinary statement "but in a more round-about way." That does not mean misunderstandings are not possible in ordinary language. Misunderstandings are an everyday occurrence. But the answer to these problems is not the construction of a logically perfect notation; it is rather the mundane process of clearing up actual cases of misunderstanding by approaching the point at hand from another direction, or by further elaboration. How this will be done will be relative to the purpose at hand. Everyday failures of communication point out the difficulties, as Ricks says, not the impossibility of meaning in ordinary language. Our concern when choosing a language should be with heading off expected or actual confusion, not with trying to foreclose all conceivable misunderstanding, no matter how unlikely.

---

[72] Comment to Waismann, 12.22.1929. Quoted in Hacker, *Insight and Illusion*, p. 97.

WITTGENSTEIN AND COMMON SENSE

In his later work Wittgenstein questioned the philosophical assumptions underlying the construction of a canonical notation. By redirecting his attention to the adequate forms of meaning in everyday language he allied himself in several important respects with the tradition of common sense philosophy. In its broadest interpretation this tradition has similarly drawn attention to beliefs, forms of argument, or types of concept, that are habitually employed and trusted but on which doubt has been thrown by epistemology or formal logic. Wittgenstein, however, as early as the *Blue and Brown Books* and most definitively in *On Certainty* distanced himself from the tradition of common sense and from Moore's philosophy in particular. The ways in which he was and was not a philosopher of common sense should be spelled out.

He represented the tradition most obviously when defending everyday language against the violent reparsing entailed by analysis. "How strange" he wrote, "if logic were concerned with an 'ideal' language and not with *ours*."[73] The ideal, he found, conflicts more and more when we examine actual language, for "We see that what we call 'sentence' and 'language' has not the formal unity that I imagined, but is the family of structure more or less related to one another."[74] Adhering none the less to the requirement that logic be of "crystalline purity"[75] pushes philosophy away from what it was originally intended to clarify, until there is an unbridgeable gap opened between logical theory and most forms of thought employed in the course of life. This led to what Stephen Toulmin has called the "systematic divergence" between logical theory and our actual use of reasoning.[76] Wittgenstein confessed his own discovery of this problem:

The more narrowly we examine actual language, the sharper becomes the conflict between it and our requirement. (For the crystalline purity of logic was, of course, not a *result of investigation*: it was a requirement.) The conflict becomes intolerable; the requirement is now in danger of becoming empty. – We have got on to slippery ice where there is no

---

[73] *Philosophical Remarks*, translated by R. Hargreaves and R. White (Oxford: Basil Blackwell, 1975): p. 52.
[74] *Investigations*, sect. 108.
[75] Ibid., sect. 107.
[76] Stephen Toulmin, *The Uses of Argument* (Cambridge University Press, 1958), p. 9.

friction and so in a sense the conditions are ideal, but also, just because of that, we are unable to walk. We want to walk: so we need *friction*. Back to the rough ground![77]

Wittgenstein responded to this "systematic divergence" by "turning our whole examination round"[78] and concluding against the revisionists "that we must stick to the subjects of our everyday thinking, and not go astray and imagine that we have to describe extreme subtleties."[79] No longer believing that a single logical structure must be implicit in language, he turned instead to examine the different ways we actually go about reasoning and using words in everyday life. His distinctive contribution to the tradition of common sense is however not just a critique of the specific doctrines of analytic philosophy, but an analysis of why philosophy continually makes "shocking" statements. His new approach was to show that many philosophical problems are "grammatical illusions,"[80] confusions that arise because of mis-understandings about how our words get their meaning: "Philosophy is a battle against the bewitchment of our intelligence by means of language."[81] Where once philosophy got bogged down in conundrums arising from too narrow a conception of thought or reason Wittgenstein showed that the pseudo-problems are dissolved in the course of examining how the words in question are actually used in everyday language. This task he often likened to psycho-analysis.[82] Baker and Hacker describe this method:

Like the psychoanalyst, he merely makes the patient, the philosopher in the grip of a misguided picture, aware of what he is doing . . . Wittgenstein . . . shows how metaphysical doctrines stem from misuse of language. He arranges the grammatical rules which he elicits from the person who suffers from philosophical bafflement to reveal points of tension and to lay bare conflicting and illegitimate applications of language.[83]

---

[77] *Investigations*, sect. 107.   [78] Ibid., sect. 108.
[79] Ibid., sect. 106.   [80] Ibid., sect. 110.
[81] Ibid., sect. 109.
[82] Sections 109–33 of the *Investigations* deal with the notion of philosophy as therapy. See as well *Blue and Brown Books*, p. 59; *Philosophical Remarks*, p. 52; and *Lectures, Cambridge 1930–1932*. Edited by Desmond Lee (Totowa: Rowman and Littlefield, 1980): pp. 1, 22. Also see Charles Crittenden, "Wittgenstein on Philosophical Therapy and Under-standing," *International Philosophical Quarterly* 5 (1970), pp. 20–43.
[83] *Wittgenstein*, pp. 288–9.

Philosophy as therapy was Wittgenstein's view of the role of ordinary language philosophy.

Wittgenstein also shared the view, found in Peirce and Sidgwick, that vagueness is a characteristic feature of the habitual forms of discourse being defended. Ordinary language appears vague and tentative compared to the ideal of a canonical notation, but it is in fact more solidly grounded and more economical in serving its purposes than its putative analyzed forms. He recommended that we look and see how words function in their native contexts, because this will disabuse us of the idea that they are inadequate as is. In this respect Wittgenstein came to be in substantive agreement with Moore, who similarly reminded philosophers of the forms of unambiguous discourse already existing in natural language. Moore, long before, had criticized philosophers such as Russell for thinking that propositions such as "the earth has existed for many years," or everyday propositions concerning the objects of perception, are not fully, or obviously, true as stated, but must be reformulated before any truth in them can be displayed. For example, Russell kicked off his book, *The Problems of Philosophy*, with the following claim:

In daily life, we assume as certain many things which, on a closer scrutiny, are found to be so full of contradictions that only a great amount of thought enables us to know what it is that we really may believe . . . It seems to me that I am now sitting in a chair, at a table of a certain shape, on which I see sheets of paper with writing or print . . . Yet all this may be reasonably doubted, and all of it requires much careful discussion before we can be sure that we have stated it in a form that is wholly true.[84]

Moore, on the other hand, defended the truth of such propositions without recourse to the fully analyzed state: "I meant by each of them precisely what every reader, in reading them, will have understood me to mean."[85] And he thought that such statements, in ordinary language, are a paradigm case of philosophical certainty:

I have assumed that there is some meaning which is *the* ordinary or popular meaning of such expressions as "The earth has existed for many years past." And this, I am afraid, is an assumption which some philosophers are capable of disputing. They seem to think that the question "Do you believe that the earth has existed for many years past?"

---

[84] (London: Oxford University Press, 1912), pp. 1–2.
[85] "A Defense of Common Sense," p. 198.

is not a plain question, such as should be met either by a plain "Yes" or "No," or by a plain "I can't make up my mind," but is the sort of question which can be properly met by : "It all depends on what you mean by 'the earth' and 'exists' and 'years'" . . . It seems to me that such a view is as profoundly mistaken as any view can be. Such an expression as "The earth has existed for many years past" is the very type of unambiguous expression, the meaning of which we all understand.[86]

In their critiques of analytic philosophy, Wittgenstein and Moore thus developed defenses of ordinary forms of discourse which were in many respects quite similar. This observation has led to varying assessments of the relationship between their philosophies. It can be argued that the significant point of comparison, given the prevailing philosophy at Cambridge against which they rebelled, was, as mentioned above, their common belief that the analytic project of reconstructing our language was misconceived. Thus Wittgenstein did recognize the importance of Moore's defense of common sense. As Norman Malcolm recorded, Wittgenstein later grudgingly "admitted that Moore's 'defense of common sense' was an important idea".[87] Similarly, K. T. Fann concludes that Moore's method of "careful . . . *distinction* of ordinary usage and his persistent defense of common sense are . . . conspicuously present in Wittgenstein's later work."[88] Alice Ambrose similarly suggests that Moore may have helped turn attention towards a closer analysis of ordinary language.[89]

However, Wittgenstein, although sympathetic to Moore's intentions, was highly critical of his particular line of argument. In distinguishing his own more therapeutic philosophic approach from that of Moore, Wittgenstein wrote:

There is no common sense answer to a philosophical problem. One can defend common sense against the attacks of philosophers only by solving their puzzles, ie., by curing them of the temptation to attack common sense; not by restating the views of common sense.[90]

Wittgenstein criticised Moore for claiming to know for certain the propositions of common sense. Against the skeptic Moore used

---

[86] Ibid.
[87] *Memoir*, p. 67.
[88] *Wittgenstein's Conception of Philosophy* (Berkeley: University of California Press, 1971), p. 511.
[89] "Three Aspects of Moore's Philosophy," p. 87.
[90] *Blue and Brown Books*, pp. 58–9.

the familiar gambit of arguing that the propositions being doubted attain a certainty that the grounds for doubting them can never possess. Doubts as to the existence of the external world are laid to rest by viewing our hands, for example, and stating that we know there are two hands here. Wittgenstein's test for assessing if a statement is significant was to ask if it is meaningful to deny the proposition. Since it does not make much sense to say in Moore's position that I do not know that there are two hands here, the statement is not doing any work. His approach here is similar to the one we have seen he applied to the statement that all language is vague: a statement is used "in a typically metaphysical way" if it is used "without an antithesis." If a statement is used without a meaningful antithesis then this is an indication that the concepts involved have been removed from the flow of life, the language games, which alone give them meaning. "What *we* do is to bring words back from their metaphysical to their everyday use."[91] So when Moore said that he knew the propositions of common sense, Wittgenstein's response was to ask if the word "know" was being used properly. He pointed out that "'I know' often means: I have the proper grounds for my statement."[92] This implies that it is meaningful to doubt the statement, that we could imagine evidence that would throw doubt on it. But we cannot do this with Moore's propositions. "Grounds for *doubt* are lacking! Everything speaks in its favour, nothing against it."[93] Wittgenstein therefore concluded that it is wrong for Moore to claim to know the truth of his common sense propositions.

These criticisms have led to assessments such as the following by G. H. von Wright:

It is sometimes said that the later Wittgenstein resembles Moore. This is hardly true. Moore's and Wittgenstein's ways of thinking are in fact utterly different . . . I do not believe that there is any trace of an influence of Moore's philosophy on Wittgenstein.[94]

This is surely an overstatement. In addition to the obvious, although perhaps superficial, similarities between the two dealt with here, there is the undeniable evidence of Moore's influence in

---

[91] *Investigations*, 116.
[92] *On Certainty*, translated by Denis Paul and G. E. M. Anscombe (Oxford: Basil Blackwell, 1969), p. 18.
[93] Ibid., p. 4.
[94] "Biographical Sketch," in Malcolm, *Memoir*, p. 15

the fact that Wittgenstein devoted his final manuscript, *On Certainty*, to Moore's philosophy. Wittgenstein clearly thought Moore's position was important enough to warrant a thorough examination. Besides, Wittgenstein recognized in the propositions of common sense a species of statement that none the less retained value in arguing against Cartesian doubt. He shared with Moore the belief that these propositions were presupposed by the act of doubting employed by the skeptic. The difference between Moore's and Wittgenstein's interpretations of the logical status of the propositions can be put as follows: while Moore believed they were propositions which he could know with certainty, Wittgenstein believed that they were propositions we could not doubt. And this species of belief provides the background against which the practices of doubting and knowing take place. So Wittgenstein retained a great deal of Moore's original ideas, giving them a more subtle reading. Perhaps that is why he grudgingly admitted that Moore's defense of common sense was a good idea.

CHAPTER 3

Keynes and Moore's common sense

Many of the concepts and lines of argument that characterized later Cambridge philosophy show up in Keynes's philosophical and methodological writings from the time. He too focused on the property of vagueness and the problems it presented to the formalisation of everyday language. In the next chapter I look at Keynes's own departure from the early ideals of analytic philosophy, and at how he incorporated the new ideas into his philosophy of the social sciences. However, by first looking at Keynes's early thought, particularly some overlooked marginalia in the *Treatise on Probability*, we can see that his later position had its roots securely in Moore's common sense philosophy.

In the *Treatise on Probability* Keynes was working squarely within the analytic tradition, extending Russell's account of the logical relationship between "intuitive knowledge" and "derivative knowledge" to the realm of probable knowledge.[1] However, he expressed doubts about many of the core assumptions of analysis. The prime concern on the part of commentators with judging whether Keynes was successful in providing logical foundations for probable knowledge has drawn attention away from those aspects of his philosophy that presaged ordinary language philosophy. Looking at those aspects enables us to see that Keynes enjoyed a critical distance from the epistemic ideals informing the methods then being developed in both philosophy and economics. In Wittgenstein's later philosophy Keynes found a logical vindication of his earlier reservations, one he no longer had time to provide. As we will see when we turn to the biographical details in chapter 6, Keynes took greater interest in Wittgenstein's philosophy when their views on the problems of formalization converged. For now, by pointing out

[1] See Richard Braithwaite, Editorial Foreword, *Collected Works*, vol. 8.

Keynes's struggle with the epistemic ideals prevalent at the time of analysis one can begin to see why he prefaced the *General Theory* with the confession of "a long struggle of escape . . . from habitual modes of thought and expression."[2]

THE "TREATISE ON PROBABILITY"

In light of the development of Cambridge philosophy some of the most incisive comments of the *Treatise on Probability* are couched as asides, asides however which indicate what it was in analytic philosophy that was disturbing him at the time. Of course, Keynes undertook the project because he thought that the sole concern with demonstrative certainty had caused logic to withdraw from studying the arguments used in actual reasoning, arguments which fell short of certainty:

The course which the history of thought has led Logic to follow has encouraged the view that doubtful arguments are not within its scope. But in the actual exercise of reason we do not wait on certainty, or deem it irrational to depend on a doubtful argument. If logic investigates the general principles of valid thought, the study of arguments, to which it is rational to attach *some* weight, is as much a part of it as the study of those which are demonstrative.[3]

Regardless of the formal analysis that followed, the intention of the book was to rescue the respectability of a form of everyday thought, and this in itself is a concern that characterizes later Cambridge philosophy.

Keynes hoped to blend the logical methods of Russell with both Moore's defense of common sense and his non-utilitarian brand of ethics. Keynes later wrote: "I was writing under the joint influence of Moore's *Principia Ethica* and Russell's *Principia Mathematica*."[4] More specifically, he said: "Russell's *Principles of Mathematics* came out in the same year as *Principia Ethica*; and the former, in spirit, furnished a method for handling the material provided by the

---

2 *Collected Works*, vol. 7, p. xxiii.
3 *Collected Works*, vol. 8, p. 3.
4 *Collected Works*, vol. 10, p. 445. Russell in turn pays tribute to both Moore and Keynes: "I have derived valuable assistance from unpublished writings of G. E. Moore and J. M. Keynes: from the former, as regards the relations of sense-data to physical objects, and from the latter as regards probability and induction," *The Problems of Philosophy*, preface.

latter."[5] Indeed, Keynes recorded that it was the importance of "probability in [Moore's] theory of right conduct" that encouraged him to undertake the study.[6] He briefly returned to this issue in the *Treatise* where he claimed that Moore had "a wrong philosophical interpretation of probability," and then attempted to remedy this failure.[7] In response to Moore's comments on "our utter ignorance of the far future," Keynes said "Mr. Moore's reasoning endeavours to show that there is not even a *probability* by showing that there is not a *certainty*."[8] Robert Skidelsky explains that Moore, by accepting the impossibility of rationally estimating future consequences of our actions, was led to fall back on "the existing rules of morality."[9] The public rules contain more information than any single participant; the market for moral values, it could be said, is efficient. Keynes, on the other hand, wanted to attribute this knowledge to the individual agents. As Skidelsky argues, Keynes "wanted to show that we can make a rational probability judgment without possessing the kind of knowledge which Moore seemed to suppose we must possess before we can rationally decide for ourselves what we ought to do."[10]

Keynes also thought that the methods he was developing could be used to support Moore's defense of common sense from the attacks of the analysts. He wrote of the need for a "logical theory, which is to justify common sense,"[11] and elsewhere elaborated on the wider implications of this project for philosophy:

The conception of our having *some* reason, though not a conclusive one, for certain beliefs, arising out of direct inspection, may prove important to the theory of epistemology. The old metaphysics has been greatly hindered by reason of its having always demanded demonstrative certainty.[12]

His conception of probability pointed to a novel approach to the problems of metaphysics, and Keynes claimed that in one paper

[5] *Collected Works*, vol. 10, pp. 438–9. See also Harrod, "Note on 'Treatise on Probability,'" in *The Life of John Maynard Keynes* (London: Macmillan, 1951), pp. 651–6.
[6] *Collected Works*, vol. 10, p. 445.
[7] *Collected Works*, vol. 8, p. 342.
[8] Ibid., pp. 341–2.
[9] *John Maynard Keynes. Hopes Betrayed, 1883–1920* (London: Macmillan, 1983), p. 152.
[10] Ibid.
[11] *Collected Works*, vol. 8, p. 274. He also wrote: "It was suggested in the previous chapter that our theory of analogy ought to be as applicable to mathematical as to material generalisations, if it is to justify common sense." Ibid., p. 290.
[12] *Collected Works*, vol. 8, p. 266.

Moore "seems to me to apply for the first time a method somewhat resembling that which is described above."[13] In the mentioned article Moore tackled the issue of proving the existence of the external world by looking for reasons that merely make its existence *"highly probable:"*[14]

And I wish it to be understood that I am using the words 'reason for a belief' in this extremely wide sense. When I look for a good reason for our belief in the existence of other people, I shall not reject any proposition merely on the ground that it only renders their existence probable – only shows it to be more likely than not that they exist.[15]

In this way Moore attempted to provide grounds for his common sense beliefs without being driven to the various forms of skepticism or philosophical reconstruction which have issued from previous epistemologies. Epistemological views never drove Moore from his common sense beliefs. In conclusion to this article he wrote: "The more I look at objects round me, the more I am unable to resist the conviction that what I see does exist, as truly and as really, as my perception of it. The conviction is overwhelming."[16] Thus, Keynes suggested "When we allow that probable knowledge is, nevertheless, real, a new method of argument can be introduced into metaphysical discussions."[17]

Elsewhere Keynes doubted that analysis could provide a bedrock stratum of unambiguous discourse. He made the same point as Moore and the later Wittgenstein that the a priori dedication to Fregean precision in order to facilitate communication and understanding can turn into its opposite by producing bulky and complex discourse. In a comment on Russell's logic, for example, he suggested that the greater sophistication of technique has raised the problem of how this form of analysis is to be related to the givens of common sense which it was intended to clarify. Keynes commented:

But beyond the fact that the conclusions to which [Russell] seeks to lead up are those of common sense . . . he is not concerned with analysing the methods of valid reasoning which we actually employ. He concludes with familiar results, but he reaches them from premises, which have never

---

13 Ibid., pp. 266–7, n. 1. The article in question was "The Nature and Reality of Objects of Perception," *Proceedings of the Aristotelian Society* 6 (1906), pp. 68–127.
14 "Nature and Reality," p. 77.   15 Ibid.
16 Ibid., p. 126.   17 *Collected Works*, vol. 8, p. 266.

occurred to us before, and by an argument so elaborate that our minds have difficulty in following it . . . [I]t gives rise to questions about the relation in which ordinary reasoning stands to this ordered system.[18]

Similarly, in a footnote at the end of his chapter on the theory of knowledge, he criticized the reductionist symbolism of *Principia Mathematica*, and questioned in what sense it was preferable to everyday language in exposing fallacious reasoning:

Confusion of thought is not always best avoided by technical and unaccustomed expressions, to which the mind has no immediate reaction of understanding; it is possible, under the cover of a careful formalism, to make statements, which, if expressed in plain language, the mind would immediately repudiate. There is much to be said, therefore, in favour of understanding the substance of what you are saying *all the time*, and of never reducing the substantives of your argument to the mental status of an x or y.[19]

Keynes cast doubt on the putative universal efficiency of symbolism; and he also went further by suggesting that rather than being a more sure-footed route for inquiry to follow, a symbolic treatment could disguise faulty reasoning. Later in the *Treatise* he provided an example of this obfuscation, an example which was repeated later on numerous occasions when criticizing classical economists for trying to reduce uncertain knowledge to the status of practical certainty.[20] He considered the idea that

we can attribute a definite measure to our future expectations and can claim practical certainty for the results of predictions which lie within relatively narrow limits. Coolly considered, this is a preposterous claim, which would have been universally rejected long ago, if those who made it had not so successfully concealed themselves from the eyes of common sense in a maze of mathematics.[21]

In these early passages Keynes expressed a doubt that analysis, or the reduction of everyday language to the symbolism of logic, is the best means of achieving consensus and aiding understanding. The passages also indicate the difficulty he had in combining the methods of Russell with Moore's defense of common sense. It was in the context of voicing these doubts that he wrote that "There are

---

[18] Ibid. p. 128.   [19] Ibid. p. 20, n. 1.
[20] See *Collected Works*, vol. 7, ch. 12; *Collected Works*, vol. 14, pp. 112–19.
[21] *Collected Works*, vol. 8, p. 424.

occasions for very exact methods of statement, such as are employed in Mr. Russell's *Principia Mathematica*. But there are advantages also in writing the English of Hume. Mr. Moore has developed in *Principia Ethica* an intermediate style which in his hands has force and beauty."[22] In the *Treatise* he hoped a reconciliation of the two methods was possible, although the above quoted passages indicate that he had more doubts about the validity of Russell's method than of Moore's. These doubts later developed into a repudiation of many of the central tenets of analytic philosophy.

Keynes also indicated his discomfort with several other aspects of the reductionism of analytic philosophy. For example, although he did not spend much time on "questions of epistemology to which I do not know the answer,"[23] he did briefly pay lip-service to the distinction between "direct and indirect knowledge,"[24] but then only to question it. The analytics sought a reduction of complex entities to the basic units of which the world is comprised, or which comprise our direct knowledge of it. Wittgenstein later criticized the notion of direct acquaintance by pointing out that we can only specify the contents of sensation once an interpretative framework of language is in place. Keynes recognized the problem when he wrote "as to when we are knowing propositions about sense data directly and when we are interpreting them – it is not possible to give a clear answer."[25] He reiterated this concern later when looking into the grounds we have for accepting the assumption of limited independent variety in justifying induction: he claimed that "so long as our knowledge of the subject of epistemology is in so disordered and undeveloped a condition as it is at present" there has not been a "proper answer . . . to the inquiry – of what sorts of things are we *capable* of direct knowledge?"[26] Keynes, perhaps to his credit, did not attempt a solution, but only recorded his doubts.

Closely related to his doubt about the immediacy of direct knowledge was the difficulty he encountered when attempting to justify the atomic hypothesis. When discussing "what the mathematicians call the principle of the super-imposition of small effects, or . . . the *atomic* character of natural law"[27] he said:

---

[22] Ibid. p. 20, n. 1.   [23] Ibid., p. 10.
[24] Ibid., p. 14.   [25] Ibid.
[26] Ibid., p. 291.   [27] Ibid., p. 276.

The system of the material universe must consist, if this kind of assumption is warranted, of bodies which we may term . . . *legal atoms,* such that each of them exercises its own separate, independent, and invariable effect, a change of the total state being compounded of a number of separate changes each of which is solely due to a separate portion of the preceding state.[28]

The atomic hypothesis was adopted by analytic philosophy in its early stages because it was the form of metaphysics with which the philosophers reacting against Bradley's and McTaggart's Idealism had tried to combat the theory that an entity could be understood only through its relations to the whole of reality.[29] Against the notion of an organic whole, the analytics, at least Russell and the early Wittgenstein, posited logical atoms as the substratum of reality, atoms moreover which were independent of each other. Thus, Wittgenstein in the *Tractatus* claimed that "Objects are simple";[30] and "States of affairs are independent of one another."[31] Keynes, on the other hand, while not holding to Bradley's Idealism, suggested the possibility of emergent properties:

Yet there might well be quite different laws for wholes of different degrees of complexity, and laws of connection between complexes which could not be stated in terms of laws connecting individual parts. In this case natural law would be organic and not, as it is generally supposed, atomic.[32]

Such a state of affairs would present difficulties for science:

If every configuration of the universe were subject to a separate and independent law, or if very small differences between bodies – in their shape or size, for instance, – led to their obeying quite different laws, prediction would be impossible and the inductive method useless.[33]

---

[28] Ibid., pp. 276–7.

[29] For a discussion of the influence of Idealism on Cambridge philosophy see Derek Crabtree, "Cambridge Intellectual Currents of 1900," in *Keynes and the Bloomsbury Group,* edited by Derek Crabtree and A. P. Thirlwall (London: Macmillan, 1980), pp. 3–21. Keynes, he points out, also felt the influence of McTaggart: "That the freshman Keynes should persuade fellow students to attend the course of lectures on general philosophy which McTaggart repeated over a number of years must be taken as . . . forceful testimony to his intellectual appeal" (p. 8) Wittgenstein indicated his disdain for Hegelianism when he wrote "The syntax of ordinary language . . . does not in all cases prevent the construction of nonsensical pseudopropositions" such as "'the Real, though it is an *in itself,* must also be able to become a *for myself.*'" ("Some Remarks on Logical Form," p. 162).

[30] *Tractatus,* 2.02.   [31] *Tractatus,* 2.061.   [32] *Collected Works,* vol. 8, p. 277.

[33] Ibid. Recently, however, the Santa Fe Institute has taken up the issue of modelling complex phenomena, both natural and social. See for example, *The Economy as an Evolving*

Keynes, while recognizing this possibility, did not accept a more organic conception of nature in the *Treatise*. In fact, when examining the assumptions required for justifying the process of induction, he proposed the assumption of limited independent variety, by which he meant that the objects of our universe "do not have an infinite number of independent qualities";[34] and this assumption he found entailed a form of atomism:

The hypothesis of atomic uniformity, as I have called it, while not formally equivalent to the hypothesis of the limitation of independent variety, amounts to very much the same thing. If the fundamental laws of connection changed altogether with variations, for instance, in the shape or size of bodies, or if the laws governing the behaviour of a complex had no relation whatever to the laws governing the behaviour of its parts when belonging to other complexes, there could hardly be a limitation of independent variety in the sense in which this has been defined. And, on the other hand, a limitation of independent variety seems necessarily to carry with it some degree of atomic uniformity. The underlying conception as to the character of the system of nature is in each case the same.[35]

He concluded his book by claiming that the validity of induction, upon which "the boasted knowledge of modern science depends," can only be maintained "if the universe of phenomena does in fact present those peculiar characteristics of atomism and limited variety."[36]

Keynes thus accepted the assumption of atomism in his justification of induction. However, from our point of view, the interesting aspect of his atomism is the absence of dogmatism about the matter. To begin with, he avoided saying anything definite about the nature of these atoms, but comments simply that "we do habitually assume . . . that the size of the atomic unit is . . . an object small in relation to our perception."[37] Furthermore, his argument has merely identified those assumptions required if the validity of induction is accepted. But Keynes could find no epistemological grounds for the assumption, candidly admitting that these are grounds which "still [elude] the peering eyes of philosophy."[38] And while accepting the assumption as necessary for

Complex System, edited by Philip Anderson, Kenneth Arrow, and David Pines (Redwood City, Calif.: Addison-Wesley, 1988).
[34] *Collected Works*, vol. 8, p. 285.
[35] Ibid., p. 290.   [36] Ibid., p. 468.
[37] Ibid., p. 278.   [38] Ibid., p. 294.

the natural sciences, he none the less held a more pluralistic view of the world than the other analytics; he did recognize that the "assumption, that *all* systems of fact are finite" is not "applicable to every kind of object and to all possible experiences."[39] Thus, he concluded, "there may be some kinds of objects . . . to which inductive methods are not applicable."[40] At this stage he mentioned only one realm of experience in which the assumptions underlying induction may not be warranted, and to which "empirical methods" are inapplicable – metaphysics.[41] However, elsewhere when dealing with Moore's analysis of organic unity he included in this category of experience both ethical notions and the contents of consciousness.

Later in his career, Keynes focused on another realm of experience in which the assumptions of atomism were not justified, and therefore one in which empirical methods would confront phenomena which displayed unanalysable complexity – that portion of the economic system which is governed primarily by expectations concerning an uncertain future. Keynes thought the properties of atomism were not displayed by psychic phenomena, and this point he drew on when later he engaged Jan Tinbergen in debate over the use of econometrics for studying the business cycle. He there reiterated, for the use of multiple correlation, the necessity of an atomistic subject matter:

If we were dealing with the action of numerically measurable, independent forces, adequately analysed so that we knew we were dealing with independent atomic factors and between them completely comprehensive, acting with fluctuating relative strength on material constant and homogeneous through time, we might be able to use the method of multiple correlation with some confidence for disentangling the laws of their action.[42]

Keynes objected to the use of econometrics for studying the business cycle because the method was being applied to "unanalysed economic material, which we know to be non-homogeneous through time."[43] I return to deal with Keynes's divergence from atomism when dealing with consciousness presently, and to his analysis of expectations in chapter 5. For the

---

[39] Ibid., p. 291.
[40] Ibid., p. 293.   [41] Ibid.
[42] *Collected Works*, vol. 14, p. 286.   [43] Ibid.

moment I wanted to point out Keynes's highly qualified acceptance of atomism, and his vision of experience wherein this property is not present.

PHENOMENOLOGY AND ORGANIC UNITY

Keynes may not have accepted an organic vision of the natural world in the *Treatise*, but elsewhere he displayed his adherence to the related notion, derived from Moore, of organic unity, a notion which is fundamentally opposed to many implications of atomism. The idea of organic unity was discussed primarily when dealing with ethical questions, although it was also considered to be a property which inhered in any meaningful entity. The challenge this property presented for ethical theory was similar to that presented to science by the prospect of an organic natural world. When discussing ethical questions, he considered

the alternatives, that either the goodness of the whole universe throughout time is organic or the goodness of the universe is the arithmetic sum of the goodnesses of infinitely numerous and infinitely divided parts.[44]

Keynes said that the "case is parallel to the question, whether physical law is organic or atomic,"[45] but he also suggested that the alternatives "are not exhaustive."[46]

I will not delve into these questions of ethical theory, as I want to concentrate on more epistemological and logical issues.[47] It is enough to have introduced these two notions of Keynes's – organic unity and an organic conception of reality. The two are distinct in that the former concerns itself with the nature of concepts, while the latter is a metaphysical position concerning the fundamental constituents of the world. However, they are related in the sense that both notions imply that the reality of the objects in question are inaccessible through an atomistic approach. In its wider application outside ethics, the notion of organic unity challenged several reductivist and atomistic assumptions within analytic philosophy.

The influence of Moore's *Principia Ethica* on the early Keynes has been amply documented in the latter's essay "My Early Beliefs,"

---

[44] *Collected Works*, vol. 8, p. 343.   [45] Ibid.
[46] Ibid.
[47] See Skidelsky, *Keynes. Hopes Betrayed*, ch. 6. This chapter provides an excellent discussion of Keynes's ethical theory and his involvement with Moore's notion of organic unity.

and by many commentators as well. What is often missing, however, is a recognition of the larger philosophical context within which both Moore and Keynes were working. The position adhered to at that time, if we are to see it as a particular instance of a general philosophical movement, which it was, was essentially phenomenological. Continental phenomenology had a direct influence, through Frege, on the Cambridge logicians, and, through Franz Brentano, on Moore's ethics. It constituted a reaction against the empiricism prevailing at the end of the nineteenth century, particularly that of John Stuart Mill. The cornerstone of this empiricism was the belief that the human mind consisted of several psychological laws operating on the givens of sensation. Phenomenology's fundamental tenet, in contrast, was that consciousness cannot be reduced to, or explained by, or understood by, empirical laws. Frege, along with Edmund Husserl, reacted against the psychologism of Mill by pointing out that the laws of logic are timelessly true, and thus cannot be explained by empirical analysis as mere psychological propensities. The Cambridge logicians made a similar break from psychologism. Wittgenstein in the *Tractatus* wrote, "Psychology is no more closely related to philosophy than any other natural science."[48] Keynes also indicated his departure from empiricism when he distinguished his logic from the earlier one where "*certainty* is . . . used in a merely psychological sense to describe a state of mind without reference to the logical grounds of the belief."[49] In criticizing Hume, he did admit that "judgments of probability . . . undoubtably depend on a strong psychological propensity in us," but goes on to point out that this is not sufficient to account for their truth:

But this is no ground for supposing that they are nothing more than "lively imaginations." The same is true of the judgments in virtue of which we assent to other logical arguments; and yet in such cases we believe that there may be present some element of objective validity, transcending the psychological impulse, with which primarily we are presented.[50]

For Keynes "the objective character of relations of probability" is grasped by "direct judgment."[51] He nicely summarized the lines of debate in a letter to C. D. Broad:

---

[48] *Tractatus*, 4.1121.   [49] *Collected Works*, vol. 8, p. 15.
[50] Ibid., p. 56.   [51] Ibid.

But what I really attach importance to is, of course, the general philosophical theory. I am much comforted that you are in general agreement. But I find that Ramsey and other young men at Cambridge are quite obdurate, and still believe that *either* Probability is a definitely measurable entity, probably connected with Frequency, *or* is of merely psychological importance and is definitely non-logical. I recognise that they can raise some very damaging criticisms against me on these lines. But all the same I feel great confidence that they are wrong. However, we shall never have the matter properly cleared up until a big advance has been made in the treatment of Probability in relation to the theory of Epistemology as a whole.[52]

Keynes's belief in the non-psychological nature of probability remained even when his book was to come under criticism from philosophers such as Frank Ramsey; and, while later grudgingly entertaining the possibility that "the basis of our degrees of belief ... is part of our human outfit, perhaps given us merely by natural selection, analogous to our perceptions and our memories rather than to formal logic," holds firm in his earlier belief: "It is not getting to the bottom of the principle of induction merely to say that it is a useful mental habit."[53]

Similarly, Moore accused empiricism, or more exactly its ethical progeny, utilitarianism, of committing a naturalistic fallacy in reducing ethical judgments to their origin in the physical elements of pleasure and pain.[54] As Keynes later recorded "we were amongst the first of our generation ... to escape from the Benthamite tradition."[55] Ethical notions for Moore were, as Keynes put it, "a matter of direct inspection, of direct unanalysable intuition."[56] In this respect Moore wanted to retain the objectivity of ethical entities. To make the point that "'good' denotes a simple and indefinable quality,"[57] Moore compared the property to another primitive quality:

---

[52] Letter of 1/31/22, *Keynes Papers*, King's College Library, Cambridge, TP/1/1, Box 18.

[53] *Collected Works*, vol. 10, p. 339. Ramsey had argued that induction, like memory and perception, is "one of the ultimate sources of knowledge," and that asking for a proof of its reliability is "to cry for the moon." "Truth and Probability," in *The Foundations of Mathematics and other Logical Essays*, edited by R. B. Braithwaite (London: Routledge & Kegan Paul, 1931), p. 197.

[54] Moore, *Principia Ethica* (Cambridge University Press, 1903) p. 10.

[55] *Collected Works*, vol. 10, p. 445. He also wrote about the Benthamite tradition: "I do now regard that as the worm which has been gnawing at the insides of modern civilisation and is responsible for its present moral decay," ibid.

[56] Ibid., p. 437.   [57] Moore, *Principia*, p. 10.

Consider yellow, for example. We may try to define it, by describing its physical equivalent; we may state what kind of light-vibrations must stimulate the normal eye, in order that we may perceive it. But a moment's reflection is sufficient to shew that those light-vibrations are not themselves what we mean by yellow. *They* are not what we perceive.[58]

He went on to argue that "a mistake of this simple kind has commonly been made about 'good,'"[59] such as equating good with pleasure, or living in accordance with natural law. The theories which have so defined our ethical notions, Moore called 'naturalistic':

This method consists in substituting for "good" some one property of a natural object or of a collection of natural objects; and in thus replacing Ethics by some one of the natural sciences . . . In general, Psychology has been the science substituted, as by J. S. Mill . . . [60]

These attempts at scientific ethics have committed the naturalistic fallacy, and are the object of Moore's phenomenological criticisms.

In *Principia Ethica* Moore combined certain aspects of analysis with a core assumption of phenomenology, which might be summarised by saying that for the givens of consciousness the whole is more than the sum of the parts. On the one hand, he accepted that there are entities which are "simple and [have] no parts";[61] are "simple and indefinable";[62] and are "the ultimate terms"[63] of definition, such as yellow and good. On the other, he believed these entities could enter into an "organic" whole, by which he meant that the "whole has an intrinsic value different in amount from the sum of the values of its parts."[64] Moore thought that complex entities could be built up from simple objects, and that the meaning or value of these wholes is not simply the additive values of the constituent parts; in Keynes's words "their value depended, in accordance with the principle of organic unity, on the state of affairs as a whole which could not be usefully analysed into parts."[65] So, for Moore, the reduction of ethical judgments, or the reduction of perception, to an atomic substratum violated the

[58] Ibid.
[59] Ibid. Keynes similarly wrote: "Our apprehension of good was exactly the same as our apprehension of green, and we purported to handle it with the same logical and analytical technique which was appropriate to the latter." *Collected Works*, vol. 10, p. 438.
[60] Ibid. p. 40.   [61] Ibid., p. 9.
[62] Ibid., p. 10.   [63] Ibid.
[64] Ibid., p. 36.   [65] *Collected Works*, vol. 10, p. 436.

organic unity of ideas. Such an approach would never issue in an understanding of the concepts, just as a reduction of a painting to the quantity and color of paint used could never account for its meaning. Belief in the organic unity of ideas put Moore in the same position as the phenomenologists in that his world of ideas became a world of independently subsisting entities, ones which had to be understood on their own terms, in their uniqueness. Hence the importance of being able to describe precisely the idea being held in the mind, an activity at which Moore excelled: as Norman Malcolm recounts, Wittgenstein "observed that if one were trying to find exactly the right words to express a fine distinction of thought, Moore was absolutely the best person to consult."[66] So for Moore, as Keynes was to record, the phenomenological contents of consciousness, be they an awareness of love or beauty or truth or tables and chairs, "took on the same definition of outline, the same stable, solid, objective qualities and common-sense reality."[67]

Other analytic philosophers, however, while accepting the phenomenological account of logic, of logical relations, took the atomic approach in accounting for perception. Keynes sided with Moore in believing in the logical impossibility of reducing the contents of consciousness to its putative atomic constituents. In his 1926 essay on Edgeworth he is explicit on this matter:

The atomic hypothesis which has worked so splendidly in physics breaks down in psychics. We are faced at every turn with the problems of organic unity, of discreteness, of discontinuity – the whole is not equal to the sum of the parts, comparisons of quantity fail us, small changes produce large effects, the assumptions of a uniform and homogeneous continuum are not satisfied.[68]

---

[66] *Memoir*, p. 67.
[67] *Collected Works*, vol. 10, p. 444. Keynes referred to Moore's practice of analyzing the contents of consciousness as a form of Platonic contemplation: "They consisted in time-less, passionate states of contemplation and communion, largely unattached to 'before' and 'after,'" ibid., p. 436. This method bears a similarity to that used by Edmund Husserl. He too attempted to grasp the meaning of concepts in themselves, without reduction to the primitives of sense data, something he believed committed a "Genetic Fallacy," similar to Moore's Naturalistic Fallacy, in so far as meaning is held to inhere in the origin of perception. Husserl's method was borrowed from Descartes's method of radical doubt: by "bracketing existence," i.e., suspending all experiential associations with a concept, its timeless and objective meaning is "disclosed" in a moment of lucid and indubitable insight. cf. *Cartesian Meditations*, translated by Dorion Cairns (The Hague: Nijhoff, 1969). Husserl's philosophy, like Moore's, is also considered to be a form of Neoplatonism because it involves the belief in timeless and objective meanings.
[68] *Collected Works*, vol. 10, p. 262.

This view of the nature of consciousness was important for Keynes's later analysis of expectations. His ideas on the contrast between organic and atomic phenomena carried over into more than his analysis of expectations. They also led to his recognition that complex structures cannot always be explained through an analysis of their parts. This indeed became an important aspect of the method of the *General Theory*. He there criticized "the classical theory" for attempting to extend its analysis "of a particular industry to industry as a whole":[69] "I argue that important mistakes have been made through extending to the system as a whole conclusions which have been correctly arrived at in respect of a part of it taken in isolation."[70] There is no doubt something in the similarity between his early doubts about the universal applicability of the atomic hypothesis and his later method for dealing with more complex economic phenomena. But for the moment I would say that focusing on the notion of organic unity, or the organic nature of social reality, is to focus on the aspects of social phenomena which led Keynes to believe that mechanistic models were inappropriate; it does not by itself tell us much about his own choice of language and method for theorizing about this complexity.[71]

To sum up, while Keynes had early in his career paid homage to both Russell and Moore, it is apparent that he had serious reservations about Russell's form of analysis, and was more naturally allied with Moore's common sense philosophy. This showed itself in Keynes's fundamental reservations about (1) the assumption that reductive symbolic analyses are more precise, or less prone to ambiguity, than everyday language; (2) the possibility of specifying sense data without interpretation; and (3) the possibility of reducing complex entities to the level of simples. During the

---

[69] *Collected Works*, vol. 7, p. 260.

[70] Ibid., p. xxxii.

[71] For accounts that stress Keynes's organic vision of the economy, see Anna Carabelli, "Keynes on Cause, Chance and Possibility," in *Keynes' Economics: Methodological Issues* , edited by Tony Lawson and Hashem Pesaran (London: Croom Helm, 1985); and Allan G. Gruchy, "The Philosophical Basis of the New Keynesian Economics," Ethics 58 (July 1948), pp. 235–44. Gruchy displays the similarity of Keynes's economic approach to several strands of contemporary philosophy, the first of which "may be described as organismal, synthetic, or holistic." In addition he points out "a second important feature of modern philosophical thought which emphasizes the emergent nature of things"; and third, the "realistic or pragmatic flavour" of contemporary thought, p. 236.

thirties, however, Keynes grew critical of much of Moore's Platonism, and in the few philosophical writings from the period he sounds increasingly Wittgensteinian in his views on language. In the next chapter I look at how the seeds of Keynes's common sense later grew into a philosophical position quite distant from Moore's phenomenology, for he, along with Wittgenstein, came to believe that the property of vagueness challenged much of analysis and phenomenology.

CHAPTER 4

Keynes's later views on vagueness and definition

VAGUENESS AND MOORE'S PHENOMENOLOGY

There were several problems with Moore's phenomenology. The process of holding a concept before the mind for direct inspection ran into the same difficulties Wittgenstein had encountered when trying to specify logical atoms as the substratum of reality. Both were attempts to specify an indubitable intuition. But no intuition carries its own meaning, independent of an interpretive framework. There is, from this point of view, no difference between the analytics' recourse to referents, or images, or pictures, or whatever, and Moore's retreat to the phenomenological givens of consciousness. True, Moore's view had the sophistication of not attempting the reduction of consciousness to the atomic level. But it has not escaped Wittgenstein's criticism of all attempts to account for meaning which involve conjuring before the mind an image. Not only can we then question the source of the meaning of this image, as is done in the third man argument, but the whole endeavor implies that meaning is a mental state which accompanies the use of a word, whereas, as Wittgenstein demonstrated, meaning is displayed only in the act of doing things with words. Wittgenstein, in conversation with Norman Malcolm, mockingly described Moore's philosophical method:

Moore would like to stare at a house that is only 20 feet away and say, with a peculiar intonation, "I *know* that *there's* a *house!*" He does this because he wants to produce in himself the feeling of knowing. He wants to exhibit *knowing for certain* to himself. In this way he has the idea that he is replying to the skeptical philosopher who claims that everyday examples of knowing . . . are not really or strictly knowledge, are not knowledge *in the highest degree.*[1]

---

[1] Malcolm, *Memoir*, p. 87–8.

The form of knowing Moore was trying to attain has no real function. Wittgenstein advanced the thesis that nothing need occur in the mind when using a word, or when displaying our ability to know something. Meaning and understanding are not mental states – they are abilities to do something, and no referents, images, or phenomenological entities by themselves can guide us in a correct performance. We are taught the correct usage through training, example by example, until we can carry on by ourselves to use the word in appropriate and novel situations: Wittgenstein, in *On Certainty* wrote:

Giving grounds, however, justifying the evidence, comes to an end; – but the end is not certain propositions' striking us immediately as true, ie. it is not a kind of *seeing* on our part; it is our *acting*, which lies at the bottom of the language-game.[2]

Wittgenstein thus denied the possibility of the central meaning giving act of Moore's phenomenology.

A phenomenological approach to the specification of meaning also runs into difficulties if the concepts under study are inherently vague. In this case it becomes impossible to attain a precise understanding of the concepts in a manner hoped for by phenomenologists. While Moore thought one could get a clear understanding of our everyday concepts, could employ in our philosophical activities what Janik and Toulmin term "a refined lexicography,"[3] Wittgenstein came to doubt that definition lies at the heart of language learning and use. He made this point, possibly alluding to Moore's ethics, with the analogy of drawing an exact picture of a blurred one:

And if we carry this comparison still further it is clear that the degree to which the sharp picture *can* resemble the blurred one depends on the latter's degree of vagueness. For imagine having to sketch a sharply defined picture "corresponding" to a blurred one . . . And this is the position you are in if you look for definitions corresponding to our concepts in aesthetics or ethics.[4]

Vagueness thus threatened phenomenology, as it did analytic philosophy, for it made the precise sciences they hoped for difficult. In place of Moore's form of phenomenology as a defense of the

---

[2] Wittgenstein, *On Certainty*, para 204.
[3] *Wittgenstein's Vienna*, p. 211.   [4] *Investigations*, sect. 77.

unanalyzability of common sense and ordinary language emerged the notion of the irreducible vagueness of natural language. This line of argument had a greater influence on Keynes.

Keynes abandoned much of what was central to his and Moore's earlier philosophies, as is evident by the amused tone adopted in his essay "My Early Beliefs," wherein he surveyed his youthful enthusiasms.[5] He there made light of the Cambridge philosophers' attempts to attain certainty in their ethical judgments and complete precision in their discourse. When properly holding a concept before the mind it was, he said, "useless and impossible to argue" about the idea.[6] In the event of a disagreement it was proposed that "the two parties . . . were not bringing their intuitions to bear on precisely the same object, and, by virtue of the principle of organic unity, a very small difference in the object might make a very big difference in the result."[7] Alternatively, "victory was with those who could speak with the greatest appearance of clear, undoubting conviction and could best use the accents of infallibility."[8] These humorous comments are, in fact, a perfectly valid critique of phenomenology, for it is not clear how one is to communicate, and argue about, ideas which are intuited. Indeed, Ramsey made this criticism of Keynes's account of the objective nature of probability relations, pointing out that the rationality of a probability judgment could only be established through argument, and not by the parties concerned attending to the same evidence. Richard Braithwaite, commenting on the fate of Cambridge phenomenology, including that of Keynes, pointed out:

most present-day logicians would be chary of using such verbs as "perceive" to describe knowledge of logical-consequence relationships: many would instead describe such knowledge in terms of the structure and use of language systems. They would be even more chary of claiming to perceive probability relationships.[9]

---

[5] It has been argued that Keynes's portrayal of Moore and his followers in this essay was too simplistic, and in many ways unfair. Skidelsky points out "Some argued that Moore's doctrine could not have been so naive as Keynes made it out to be; others that Keynes's beliefs could not have been so naive as his account makes them appear," *John Maynard Keynes: The Economist as Saviour, 1920–1937* (London: Macmillan, 1942), p. 143. Pages 143–7 survey these criticisms.

[6] *Collected Works*, vol. 10, p. 437.

[7] Ibid.   [8] Ibid., p. 438.

[9] "Keynes as a Philosopher," in *Essays on John Maynard Keynes*, edited by Milo Keynes (Cambridge University Press, 1975), p. 240.

After the *Treatise on Probability* Keynes made little mention of the phenomenological side of his theory.

Other comments in the essay show that Keynes had absorbed some of Wittgenstein's new philosophy:

It was all under the influence of Moore's method, according to which you could hope to make essentially vague notions clear by using precise language about them and asking exact questions. It was a method of discovery by the instrument of impeccable grammar and an unambiguous dictionary.[10]

Looking back at these days from the vantage point of 1938, Keynes indicated the great change that had come about in his philosophical beliefs when he wrote that "it is a comfort to-day to be able to discard with a good conscience the calculus and the mensuration and the duty to know exactly what one means and feels."[11] In this essay he indicated that he had moved beyond Moore's philosophy. He, along with Wittgenstein, recognized that many of the key concepts in philosophy, ethics, and the social sciences, are, as he wrote, "essentially vague notions."

VAGUE CONCEPTS AND THE GENERAL THEORY

During the transition to the *General Theory* Keynes increasingly used the term "vagueness" when writing about economic concepts. He casually referred to the concept earlier in the *Treatise on Probability*. But he there employed the term in a variety of ways, which indicates that it was not a concept of central concern to him at that time. At one point he does employ the term synonymously with non-quantitative:

There is a vagueness, it may be noticed, in the number of instances, which would be required on the above assumptions to establish a given numerical degree of probability, which corresponds to the vagueness in the degree of probability which we do actually attach to inductive conclusions.[12]

He did accept the analytics' characterization of it as a property that vitiates thought:

---

[10] *Collected Works*, vol. 10, p. 440.
[11] Ibid., p. 442. [12] *Collected Works*, vol. 8, p. 288.

I cannot attempt here to analyse the meaning of vague knowledge. It is certainly not the same thing as knowledge proper, whether certain, or probable, and it does not seem likely that it is susceptible of strict logical treatment. At any rate I do not know how to deal with it, and in spite of its importance I will not complicate a difficult subject by endeavouring to treat adequately the theory of vague knowledge.[13]

At that point, then, he had little to say about vagueness, and he accepted the prevailing view that it is the antithesis of knowledge. Indeed, he, along with the other analytics, considered that "The object of a logical system of probability is to enable us . . . to convert . . . vague knowledge into more distinct knowledge."[14]

During the thirties, however, the word crept into several of Keynes's manuscripts, and he began to use it in much the same way as Wittgenstein. He there focused on the vagueness of concepts in the social sciences. This was an important point during the transition to the *General Theory*, for he found a close connection between his new theory and the language in which it was couched. In Book Two, which deals "with certain general problems of method and definition,"[15] he explained that the lengthy treatment of definition was required because two of the "perplexities which most impeded my progress in writing this book, so that I could not express myself conveniently until I had found some solution for them" were "the choice of the units of quantity appropriate to the problems of the economic system as a whole" and "the definition of income."[16] He later added:

I occupied much space in the first half of my book by analyses and definitions of income, saving, investment and other such terms. The excuse and explanation of this are to be found in the widespread confusion which has surrounded these terms in recent discussions, and the subtlety of the points involved. I felt that I had to try to clear the matter up to the best of my ability.[17]

Furthermore, much of his early lectures, prefaces, and drafts for the *General Theory* dwelt on questions of definition, method, and form of argument appropriate for an economic analysis of the economic system as a whole. These were written to address the belief that it is only within symbolic models that concepts can be

[13] Ibid., pp. 17–18.   [14] Ibid., p. 57.
[15] *Collected Works*, vol. 7, p. 89.
[16] Ibid., p. 37.   [17] *Collected Works*, vol. 14, p. 212.

given a precise meaning. Keynes's arguments and choice of words in these passages correspond to a remarkable degree to those being employed at the same time by Wittgenstein in his critique of analytic philosophy's ideal language. In the *Philosophical Remarks*, written around the beginning of the thirties, Wittgenstein wrote:

The moment we try to apply exact concepts of measurement to immediate experience, we come up against a peculiar vagueness in this experience. But that only means a vagueness relative to these concepts of measurement. And, now, it seems to me that this vagueness isn't something provisional, to be eliminated later on by more precise knowledge, but that this is a characteristic logical peculiarity.[18]

This point is echoed in one of the early proofs of Book Two of the *General Theory*. When explaining that problems of definition must be dealt with because they do "not happen to have been already treated elsewhere in a way which I find adequate to the needs of my own particular enquiry,"[19] Keynes criticized formal methods in much the same words as Wittgenstein:

Much economic theorising to-day suffers, I think, because it attempts to apply highly precise and mathematical methods to material which is itself much too vague to support such treatment.[20]

Because of this feature of economic reality, he concluded, "Our precision will be a mock precision if we try to use such partly vague and non-quantitative concepts as the basis of a quantitative analysis."[21]

Keynes did not think this vagueness was troublesome for he and Wittgenstein meant by the term merely that much of experience is not reducible to the primitives of mathematics or logic: they meant "a vagueness relative to these concepts of measurement." Keynes made clear his use of the term in his discussion of the units of quantity. He found the treatment of units of quantity in other economists unsatisfactory because of their attempts to quantify essentially "vague concepts, such as the quantity of output as a whole, the quantity of capital equipment as a whole and the general level of prices."[22] The national dividend, as employed by Marshall

---

[18] Edited by Rush Rhees; translated by R. Hargreaves and R. White (University of Chicago Press, 1975), p. 263.
[19] *Collected Works*, vol. 14, p. 379.   [20] Ibid.
[21] *Collected Works*, vol. 7, p. 40.   [22] Ibid., p. 43.

and Pigou, involves adding up the real income, not the money-income, of the community, and on the basis of real quantities "an attempt is made to erect a quantitative science."[23] This hope has proved a chimera for "the community's output of goods and services is a non-homogeneous complex which cannot be measured."[24] Similarly, in trying to measure the net increase in the economy's real capital stock the problems of "comparing one real output with another ... presents conundrums which permit, one can confidently say, of no solution."[25] Finally, in returning to the issue of index numbers, on which he had previously worked, he claimed that the concept of a general price level involves "the well-known, but unavoidable element of vagueness," and this makes it "very unsatisfactory for the purposes of a causal analysis."[26] Keynes in these discussions obviously intended "vagueness" to be interpreted as synonymous with "non-quantitative." Thus, in a draft of Book Two, he wrote: "My object has merely been to choose definitions . . . without running into logical difficulties and quantitative vagueness."[27] This definition of vagueness is also intended when Keynes employed the term in his analysis of the fragility of expectations, and thus their intractability for classical economic theory:

Actually, however, we have, as a rule, only the vaguest idea of any but the most direct consequences of our acts ... Thus the fact that our knowledge of the future is fluctuating, vague and uncertain, renders wealth a peculiarly unsuitable subject for the methods of classical economic theory.[28]

He classified this type of knowledge vague because "our existing knowledge does not provide a sufficient basis for a calculated mathematical expectation."[29] His concluding remark at the end of the discussion of vague concepts displays his use of the term, and his

---

23 Ibid., p. 38.
24 Ibid. See as well *Collected Works*, vol. 14, pp. 417–18, where he mentioned the "fog which has surrounded the concept of the national dividend."
25 Ibid., p. 39. See also *Collected Works*, vol. 13, p. 431, where he refers to "a problem insoluble except in special cases, of the quantitative comparison of non-homogeneous items."
26 Ibid. See also *Collected Works*, vol. 29, p. 73 where he states that "an average price per unit of output ... raises precisely the same difficulties as to a quantitative measure of a non-homogeneous complex, as does the measurement of real output itself." Volume Two of his *Treatise on Money* (*Collected Works*, vol. 6) includes his earlier thoughts on price indexes.
27 *Collected Works*, vol. 14, p. 416.
28 Ibid., p. 113.   29 *Collected Works*, vol. 7, p. 152.

belief that economic analysis can do without the "mock precision" of formal methods:[30]

Nevertheless these difficulties are rightly regarded as "conundrums." They are "purely theoretical" in the sense that they never perplex, or indeed enter in any way into, business decisions and have no relevance to the causal sequence of economic events, which are clear-cut and determinate in spite of the quantitative indeterminacy of these concepts. It is natural, therefore, to conclude that they not only lack precision but are unnecessary. Obviously our quantitative analysis must be expressed without using any quantitatively vague expressions. And, indeed, as soon as one makes the attempt, it becomes clear, as I hope to show, that one can get on much better without them.[31]

Keynes did not mean that economics has to do without quantitative units. In his choice of "fundamental units" he uses the "quantities of money-value and quantities of employment" because both can be made "homogeneous,"[32] and can therefore be given a definite measure. In this respect his analysis of vagueness in the section on units is not very controversial, for after all he was merely pointing out that some economists were trying to measure something which cannot be measured, except within fairly wide limits.[33] My point here is to elucidate his use of the word "vague" as meaning irreducible to a quantitatively exact measure. This interpretation of the word is important when turning to Keynes's treatment of vagueness in definitions, rather than units. Here his analysis is more controversial, and it introduces what is distinctive about his later philosophy of the social sciences.

Wittgenstein had stressed that the property of vagueness did not prevent us from using words in a manner perfectly suited for their purposes. Just because our everyday sentences cannot be interpreted in a manner similar to formal semantics does not mean that they are inherently prone to mislead us. Keynes moved on after his treatment of units to make this point. Moreover, he argued that one can still define terms and build simplifying models, but these

---

[30] Ibid., p. 297.
[31] Ibid., p. 39. Elsewhere he claimed that it is "a matter of considerable intellectual satisfaction that these partly insoluble difficulties of quantitative description do not arise in our causal analysis," *Collected Works*, vol. 29, p. 73.
[32] *Collected Works*, vol. 7, p. 41.
[33] He did think the three units could be used for rough descriptive or historical purposes, but that even these will depend "on some broad element of judgment rather than strict calculation," *Collected Works*, vol. 7, pp. 39–40.

must be rigorous and systematic according to standards other than mathematical ones; he wrote that his model "is not, and is not meant to be, logically watertight in the sense in which mathematics is."[34] In a series of lectures given in 1932 dealing with the core ideas of the *General Theory*, he began by discussing "The difficulty of choosing convenient terminology."[35] And in this lecture he made much the same point, "one of great practical importance to anyone who essays to write an intricate work on economics,"[36] as Wittgenstein was making at the time:

A definition can often be *vague* within fairly wide limits and capable of several interpretations differing slightly from one another, and still be perfectly serviceable and free from serious risk of leading either the author or the reader into error [original italics].[37]

This lecture is key not only to understanding the importance of language to Keynes during his transitional period, but also in providing the context for interpreting much of his criticisms of formal methods. The point he made in this passage, his highly philosophical use of the word "vague," the fact that it is italicized, shows that he was making substantially the same criticism of formalization as Wittgenstein. For Keynes here displayed an acceptance of several key Wittgensteinian notions: the idea that words have a variety of interlocking uses, each of which differs slightly from the others, but all of which bear a family resemblance to one another; the use of the term "vague" to refer to this property of words; and the understanding that vague concepts can be perfectly serviceable without being analyzed. The vagueness Keynes wrote about here is combinatory vagueness, and he appreciated how difficult it is to formalize concepts displaying this property. Furthermore, he moved on to make the same criticism as Wittgenstein of the a priori belief in the efficiency of more formalized languages. Wittgenstein, it will be remembered from the example of analyzing a statement about a broom, pointed out "This sentence, one might say, achieves the same as the ordinary one, but in a more roundabout way."[38] Keynes echoed this point:

---

[34] *Collected Works*, vol. 29, p. 38.
[35] Ibid., p. 35.   [36] Ibid., p. 36.
[37] Ibid.   [38] *Investigations*, sect. 60.

If an author tries to avoid all vagueness, and to be perfectly precise, he will become so prolix and pedantic, will find it necessary to split so many hairs, and will be so constantly diverted into an attempt to clear up some other part of the subject, that he himself may perhaps never reach the matter at hand and the reader certainly will not.[39]

He returned to the issue in his lectures of November 1933, which were addressed to the question "What degree of precision is advisable in economics?"[40] His students noted that, "on the matter of precise definition of terms, there is some question as to the utility and propriety of the scholastic exercise in trying to define terms with great precision in a subject like economics."[41] One problem is that "many economists in making their definitions so precise, make them too rigid."[42] "Another danger is that you may 'precise everything away' and be left with only a comparative poverty of meaning."[43] Here Keynes pointed out the problems that ensue from defining with an artificial precision concepts that are characterized by combinatory vagueness, for the precise definition will leave out of account too much of what we intuitively intend when using the concept. Such a problem was avoided, said Keynes, by Marshall who used loose definitions but allowed the reader to infer his meaning from "the richness of his context."[44]

It is an indication of how important Keynes found linguistic issues at the time that he kicked off this lecture series by first clearing up certain preconceptions concerning the nature of economic concepts. The same points were also expressed in the 1934 draft of a preface for the *General Theory*:

But when an economist writes in a quasi-formal style, he is composing neither a document verbally complete and exact so as to be capable of a strict legal interpretation, nor a logically complete proof . . . he never states all his premises and his definitions are not perfectly clear-cut . . . It is, I think, of the essential nature of economic exposition that it gives, not a complete statement, which, even if it were possible, would be prolix and complicated to the point of obscurity but a sample statement . . . intended to suggest to the reader the whole bundle of associated ideas, so that, if he

---

[39] *Collected Works*, vol. 29, p. 36.
[40] *Keynes's Lectures, 1932–35. Notes of a Representative Student*, edited by T. Rymes (Ann Arbor: University of Michigan Press, 1989), p. 101. This volume is a compilation of notes taken by his students.
[41] Ibid., p. 102.   [42] Ibid.
[43] Ibid.   [44] Ibid.

catches the bundle, he will not in the least be confused or impeded by the technical incompleteness of the mere words which the author has written down, taken by themselves.[45]

Later, in arguing out the *General Theory*, he responded to a criticism made by H. Townsend of his treatment of the income velocity of money, by making the same point about attempts to be perfectly precise:

I think there is something suggestive in what I have written; and were I to try to make it quite water-tight in the light of your criticisms it would become so tortuous and complicated as to be worth less perhaps than in its vaguer form.[46]

And in a letter to G.F. Shove he mentioned that it is on the issue of the degree of precision to be expected from economics that he differs from the classics:

But you ought not to feel inhibited by a difficulty in making the solution precise. It may be that a part of the error in the classical analysis is due to that attempt. As soon as one is dealing with the influence of expectations and of transitory experience, one is, in the nature of things, outside the realm of the formally exact.[47]

Finally, in one of his early lectures, when explaining his choice of method, he said that "those writers who try to be *strictly* formal generally have no substance."[48]

DEFINITIONS

Keynes thought it was necessary to preface his new theory with these philosophical comments because of "the appalling state of

---

[45] *Collected Works*, vol. 13, pp. 469–70. See also *Collected Works*, vol. 29, pp. 150–1.

[46] *Collected Works*, vol. 29, p. 246.

[47] *Collected Works*, vol. 14, p. 2.

[48] *Collected Works*, vol. 29, p. 38. Nicholas Kaldor held similar views on the nature of theoretical constructs in economics. "I called them 'stylized facts' . . . because in the social sciences, unlike the natural sciences, it is impossible to establish facts that are precise and at the same time suggestive and intriguing in their implications, and that admit of no exception," *Economics Without Equilibrium*, with a preface by James Tobin (Cardiff: University College Cardiff Press, 1985), pp. 8–9. For a survey of economists who have made use of what may be termed vague theoretical constructs, see Amartya Sen, "Description as Choice", *Oxford Economic Papers* 32 (November 1980). Sen makes the point that "approximations, metaphors, simplifications, etc., have important roles in conveying the truth," p. 354.

scholasticism into which the minds of so many economists have got."[49] He used the term "scholasticism" to refer to the prevalence of technical methods within the subject, for elsewhere, in a similar critical assessment of analytic philosophy, he referred to Russell's method as "extravagantly scholastic."[50] He thus reiterated the warning that "in writing economics one is not writing either a mathematical proof or a legal document."[51] Once these prefatory comments were made, Keynes proceeded to tackle the problems of definition in the *General Theory* by choosing a definition "which is most serviceable and least likely to lead to misunderstandings";[52] and the approach he adopted was to ground the concepts he used in ordinary usage. He considered this the most efficient and economical use of concepts for analyzing actual economic behavior. He stated that his was "an analysis which is endeavoring to keep as close as it can to the actual facts of business calculation."[53]

In a draft of the *General Theory*, after a section distinguishing between consumption and investment goods, and finished and unfinished goods, he remarked:

All these arbitrary distinctions, however, are only arbitrary in a highly *a priori* sense. For from another point of view they are not arbitrary at all, but are made (like many similar distinctions in economics) so as to correspond to our actual psychology and ways of behaving and deciding and to enable us to answer the concrete questions which are likely to be asked. If we had reason to expect that a different set of lines of division would be more appropriate to our psychology of behaviour and decision, we should have to draw them differently.[54]

And in the same draft, while recognizing that "In common parlance the term *income* is somewhat vague,"[55] decided on the proper definition in the following way:

But finally I have come to the conclusion that the use of language, which is most convenient on a balance of considerations and involves the least

[49] *Collected Works*, vol. 29, p. 150. Keynes thought it unfortunate that so much time was required to clear up definitional issues. In this letter, before complaining about the scholasticism in economics, he wrote "I am interested to hear that some of their chief difficulties were with definitions. I am not surprised, though it is extraordinarily tiresome and boring that it should be so. In my book I have deemed it necessary to go into these matters at disproportionate length, whilst feeling that this was in a sense a great pity and might divert the readers' minds from the real issues."

[50] *Collected Works*, vol. 10, p. 438.   [51] *Collected Works*, vol. 29, p. 151.
[52] *Collected Works*, vol. 14, p. 416.   [53] *Collected Works*, vol. 29, p. 88.
[54] *Collected Works*, vol. 13, p. 433.   [55] Ibid., pp. 424–5.

departure from current usage, is to call the actual sale proceeds *income* and the present value of the expected sale proceeds *effective demand*.[56]

By choosing definitions on the ground that they correspond with actual usage Keynes was formulating an ordinary language social science, one that bears a resemblance to those argued for by philosophers of hermeneutics. The concern with anchoring economic analysis in everyday language was the central concern of Book Two. Indeed, much of the discussion of definitions sounds like the type of analyses used by linguistic philosophers, examining all the different ways in which the central concepts are used in business, politics, and everyday life. Keynes recognized the value of such an endeavor when, in a letter to A. C. Pigou, he argued that

it is often useful, and indeed essential, to have articles pointing out the different senses in which a common term is used, . . . or that the same writer uses them sometimes in one sense and sometimes in another without apparently noticing.[57]

This Keynes did throughout Book Two, trying to distill from the various uses of a term a definition which involved "the least departure from current usage" – "Amidst the welter of divergent usages of terms, it is agreeable to discover one fixed point."[58] Every definition is thus chosen because it corresponded with actual usage of the terms involved. Having defined income, for example, as above he equated it with "the quantity . . . which [the entrepreneur] endeavors to maximize, i.e. to his gross profit in the ordinary sense of this term; – which agrees with common sense."[59] Later in the chapter he also defended his definition of 'net income' by referring to common practice:

It will be seen that our definition of *net income* comes very close to . . . the practices of the Income Tax Commissioners . . . For the fabric of their decisions can be regarded as the result of the most careful and extensive investigation which is available, to interpret what, in practice, it is usual to treat as net income.[60]

He recognized "that net income, being based on an equivocal criterion which different authorities might interpret differently, is not perfectly clear-cut."[61] However, when considering other

---

[56] Ibid.   [57] *Collected Works*, vol. 29, p. 178.
[58] *Collected Works*, vol. 7, p. 61.   [59] Ibid., pp. 53–4.
[60] Ibid., p. 59.   [61] Ibid., p. 60.

definitions, such as Hayek's, he pointed out that "no theoretical objection can be raised against [it] as providing a possible psychological criterion of net income."[62] But Keynes, in considering the psychology involved in justifying this definition, doubted "if such an individual exists."[63] He concluded that "The above definitions of income and of net income are intended to conform as closely as possible to common usage."[64] The advantage of this method of definition, he wrote in a draft version of the chapter, is that it "yields the definition of income which is most serviceable and least likely to lead to misunderstandings."[65]

Similarly, in dealing with "savings" he pointed out "So far as I know, everyone agrees in meaning by *saving* the excess of income over what is spent on consumption. It would certainly be very inconvenient and misleading not to mean this."[66] And then of "investment": "In popular usage it is common to mean by this the purchase of an asset, old or new, by an individual or corporation."[67] He considered the restriction of the term "to the purchase of an asset on the Stock Exchange," but countered that

we speak just as readily of investing, for example, in a house, or in a machine, or in a stock of finished or unfinished goods; and, broadly speaking, new investment, as distinguished from reinvestment, means the purchase of a capital asset of any kind out of income.[68]

Thus Keynes's "own definition is in accordance with popular usage."[69] Throughout he meant saving and investment to be "taken in their straightforward sense."[70] According to these new definitions, as opposed to those used in his *Treatise on Money*, "saving and investment are, necessarily and by definition, equal – which, after all, is in full harmony with common sense and the common usage of the world."[71]

Some of the theoretical concepts Keynes required could not be found in everyday language. For example, it is not often that one hears or uses the terms "period of production," or "user cost" in the normal course of business life. So Keynes attempted to defend the use of the concepts by arguing that they captured ideas that are

---

[62] Ibid.   [63] Ibid.
[64] Ibid.   [65] *Collected Works*, vol. 14, p. 416.
[66] *Collected Works*, vol. 7, p. 74.   [67] Ibid., pp. 74–5.
[68] Ibid., p. 75.   [69] Ibid.
[70] Ibid., p. 81.   [71] *Collected Works*, vol. 14, p. 427.

used implicitly in economic life. The period of production is defined in a way which he recognized "is not identical with the usual definition, but it seems to me to embody what is significant in the idea."[72] And in a draft of the *General Theory*, when dealing with "the loss in the value of an equipment as a result of using it to produce newly finished output,"[73] he proposed to call this quantity 'user cost', a term that is not in common usage, but which is broadly descriptive of the "opinion of businessmen."[74] He refrained from employing the term 'depreciation' as he felt it "is too full of ambiguous suggestions for its use to be convenient in this context."[75] On the other hand, "businessmen would seem to have the notion of user cost implicitly in mind, though they do not formulate it distinctly."[76]

During the development of his theory, Keynes was preoccupied with formulating an ordinary language social science. This approach, however, had roots in a tradition predating the *General Theory*. Marshall, for example, was known for his frequent comments to the effect that many errors occur "as a result of not thinking in English."[77] Keynes quoted Marshall approvingly on his assessment of technical methods: "But all that has been important in their reasonings and results has, with scarcely an exception, been capable of being described in ordinary language."[78] Keynes early on wrote of the different skills required in the natural and social sciences due to the difference in their concepts. In the same article on Marshall, originally published in 1924, he wrote:

But the amalgam of logic and intuition and the wide knowledge of facts, most of which are not precise, which is required for economic interpretation in its highest form is, quite truly, overwhelmingly difficult for those whose gift mainly consists in the power to imagine and pursue to their furthest points the implications and prior conditions of comparatively simple facts which are known with a high degree of precision.[79]

At the end of this discussion Keynes did however add that "In his reaction against excessive addiction to these methods . . . Marshall

---

[72] *Collected Works*, vol. 7, p. 287. See also *Collected Works*, vol. 29, pp. 74–5.

[73] *Collected Works*, vol. 14, pp. 400–1.   [74] *Collected Works*, vol. 7, p. 71.

[75] *Collected Works*, vol. 14, p. 400.   [76] *Collected Works*, vol. 7, p. 71.

[77] *Memorials of Alfred Marshall*, edited by A. C. Pigou (London: Macmillan, 1925), p. 428.

[78] *Collected Works*, vol. 10, p. 187.

[79] Ibid., p. 186.

may have gone too far,"[80] indicating I think his ambivalence during the twenties toward formalization.

Thus there was something of a precedent for ordinary language economics in Cambridge.[81] Keynes even had one foot in this tradition at the time of the *Treatise on Money*, for he occasionally displayed a concern with defining his terms in accordance with common usage. In considering "the variety of ways in which the term *profits* has been employed, both by economists and in business usage" he suggested "it might be better to employ the term *windfalls* for what I call *profits*."[82] He decided against the substitution, preferring "the term *profits* as carrying with it on the whole the most helpful penumbra of suggestion."[83] Indeed, he thought this important enough that he took pains to use familiar terminology, even though half way through the book he began running out of these. He remarked in a footnote: "It is difficult to decide what is the most convenient exploitation of existing non-technical language for exact technical meanings."[84] He briefly returned to this point when recommending that D. H. Robertson substitute more common expressions for his "automatic" and "induced lacking."[85]

However, there is a difference between Keynes's earlier books and the *General Theory*, for what in the *Treatise on Money*, as well as the *Treatise on Probability*, was relegated to footnotes moved to center stage as a preoccupation in developing his later ideas. In the earlier books Keynes thought his conclusions could be expressed either verbally, in familiar terms, as well as exactly using the fundamental theorems of the *Treatise on Probability* and the fundamental equations of the *Treatise on Money*. Keynes's position on the relation between the two levels of discourse was thus similar to Aristotle's view that rhetoric was the public face of dialectic, or logic. Keynes claimed that "we have found that the suggestions of common sense are supported by more precise methods."[86] And in sketching out the fundamental terms of the *Treatise on Probability* he noted:

---

[80] Ibid., p. 188.
[81] Carabelli's book, *On Keynes's Method* (London: Macmillan, 1988), is a good survey of Keynes's early preference for ordinary language.
[82] *Collected Works*, vol. 5, p. 113.
[83] Ibid., p. 113.   [84] Ibid., p. 127.
[85] Ibid., p. 154.   [86] *Collected Works*, vol. 8, p. 267.

While taking pains, therefore, to avoid any divergence between the substance of this chapter and of those which succeed it, and to employ only such periphrases as could be translated, *if desired*, into perfectly exact language, I shall not cut myself off from the convenient, but looser, expressions, which have been habitually employed by previous writers and have the advantage of being, in a general way at least, immediately intelligible to the reader.[87]

In the footnote following this passage Keynes then went on to question whether "confusion of thought" is best avoided by an unaccustomed symbolism. Just as Wittgenstein came to doubt the possibility of the translation of everyday language into symbolic logic, so too Keynes came to think that "the perfectly exact language" of the fundamental theorems and equations could not be connected with "the convenient, but looser, expressions" which are "immediately intelligible to the reader." For it is characteristic of the *General Theory* that it dispensed with almost all the equations and symbolism of the *Treatise on Money*. When, in his later book, he did turn in a discussion of the quantity theory of money to engage in a bit of symbolic manipulation, he quickly cautioned that:

I do not myself attach much value to manipulations of this kind; and I would repeat the warning . . . that they involve just as much tacit assumption as to what variables are taken as independent . . . as does ordinary discourse, whilst I doubt if they can carry us any further than ordinary discourse can. Perhaps the best purpose served by writing them down is to exhibit the extreme complexity of the relationship between prices and the quantity of money, when we express it in a formal manner.[88]

It is also characteristic of this period that his expressed doubts about formalization become a recurring motif, and that he praised ordinary language for being more efficient in handling the complexity of economic relationships.

Keynes also realized that confusion can result from an unfamiliar use of a familiar term. He criticized his *Treatise on Money* on this ground, admitting that he had "defined income in a special sense":[89]

I am afraid that this use of terms has caused considerable confusion, especially in the case of the correlative use of saving; since conclusions . . . which were only valid if the terms employed were interpreted in

---

[87] Ibid., pp. 19–20.
[88] *Collected Works*, vol. 7, p. 305.   [89] Ibid., p. 60.

my special sense, have been frequently adopted in popular discussion as though the terms were being employed in their more familiar sense.[90]

The danger of mixing up technical and common uses of words was another criticism made of the early analytics. G. A. Paul, commenting on Moore, points out the

danger inherent in giving to a simple common phrase . . . any special, as it were *technical*, meaning: the danger, namely, of slipping unawares from the special back to the ordinary; that is, of an unnoticed change, or even duplicity, of meaning, the very cause which Analytic discrimination had originally been brought in to cure.[91]

By recognizing that the symbolism and technical definitions of his earlier work merely increased confusion of thought, and by doing away with these features in his later work, doubts and insights that were only marginalia emerged, alongside Wittgenstein's later philosophy, into a defense of the efficiency of ordinary language in the social sciences.

KEYNES'S SCHEMATISM

We now have enough before us to see that the question of the appropriate language for the social sciences was of great importance to Keynes when he was formulating the *General Theory*. Furthermore his ideas on this question echoed those of Wittgenstein. Keynes fully appreciated the bewildering complexity of economic reality, and like any social scientist he had to devise a method adequate to handle this complexity. His preference for the concepts of ordinary discourse stemmed from the belief, shared with Wittgenstein, that these embody a wealth of tacit knowledge that cannot be efficiently replicated in a formal notation. This property of everyday language can for certain purposes make it paradoxically more efficient than formalized languages. Once the philosophical context of this point is sketched in one can approach some of the more cryptic philosophical passages in the *General Theory* and recognize their philosophical pedigree. In "The Theory

---

[90] Ibid., p. 61.
[91] "G. E. Moore: Analysis, Common Usage, and Common Sense," in *The Revolution in Philosophy*, edited by Gilbert Ryle (London: Macmillan, 1956), p. 64.

of Prices," for example, he indicated the need for some sort of general equilibrium approach:

The object of our analysis is . . . to provide ourselves with an organised and orderly method of thinking out particular problems; and, after we have reached a provisional conclusion by isolating the complicating factors one by one, we then have to go back on ourselves and allow, as well as we can, for the probable interactions of the factors amongst themselves. This is the nature of economic thinking.[92]

He then considered the competing methods in economics and recommended the greater efficiency of everyday language on the grounds that when using it we are not suppressing all our tacit knowledge:

It is a great fault of symbolic pseudo-mathematical methods of formalising a system of economic analysis . . . that they expressly assume strict independence between the factors involved and lose all their cogency and authority if this hypothesis is disallowed; whereas in ordinary discourse, where we are not blindly manipulating but know all the time what we are doing and what the words mean, we can keep "at the back of our heads" the necessary reserves and qualifications and the adjustments which we shall have to make later on . . . Too large a proportion of recent "mathematical" economics are merely concoctions, as imprecise as the initial assumptions they rest on, which allow the author to lose sight of the complexities and interdependencies of the real world in a maze of pretentious and unhelpful symbols.[93]

The same point that everyday language embodies far more implicit knowledge than can be made explicit in a formalized treatment is also made when summarizing the *General Theory*: after once again cautioning about "the extreme complexity of the actual course of events"[94] Keynes concluded:

If we examine any actual problem along the lines of the above schematism, we shall find it more manageable; and our practical intuition (which can take account of a more detailed complex of facts than can be treated on general principles) will be offered a less intractable material upon which to work.[95]

He returned to this methodological point when arguing out various points of the *General Theory*. He debated with Joan Robinson

---

[92] *Collected Works*, vol. 7, p. 297.   [93] Ibid., pp. 297–8.
[94] Ibid., p. 249.   [95] Ibid.

over the advantages of her more symbolic method of displaying the relationship between output and investment relative to his more verbal treatment:

Finally there is the question which is the best of two alternative exegetical methods. Here I am open to conviction. But to be convinced I should need to see the whole theory worked out your way, and then compare it with what I am able to say in my language. I am not so familiar with your way as with my own. But my present belief is that in general, and apart from the handling of certain special problems, your way would be much more difficult and cumbersome. At any rate I lack sufficient evidence to the contrary to induce me to scrap all my present half-forged weapons.[96]

He evidently did not become persuaded of the superiority of her symbolic method. And later, in correspondence with Harrod concerning an article for the *Economic Journal*, Keynes commented that the article had "some extremely interesting ideas and material in it."[97] However, he took issue with Harrod's "very muddling symbolism"[98] for obscuring "the fundamental presupposition of the whole story."[99] His criticism, "from the readers point of view" was the following:

I still find the exposition half-baked and prolix, and I have found it practically impossible to work things out for myself in terms of your symbolism, which is so contrived as to lose sight of the dimensions of your quantities, which makes it very difficult to handle.[100]

Keynes then proceeded in a few pages to state the argument in more straightforward language.

The textual evidence presented here amply illustrates the similarities between Keynes's and Wittgenstein's later views on the problems of formalizing concepts which display combinatory vagueness. Both of them penned these analyses during the early years of the thirties, a time when, as we will see, they had frequent conversations. It seems likely therefore that Keynes picked up at least part of the logical argument he employed to defend the efficiency of ordinary language from Wittgenstein. He had inherited a respect for the givens of common sense from Moore, but the arguments he had earlier used to defend its claims were found

---

[96] *Collected Works*, vol. 13, p. 378.
[97] *Collected Works*, vol. 14, p. 339.   [98] Ibid., p. 340.
[99] Ibid., p. 339.   [100] Ibid.

to be flawed. The tacit knowledge we need to draw upon in the formulation of social theory he found embodied in the vague penumbra surrounding our concepts, not in their phenomenological purity. He thus came to share with Wittgenstein a common critique of Moore's philosophy. During this period he claimed he was returning to a venerable tradition of common sense, but the arguments used to defend this approach were now drawn from later, rather than early, Cambridge philosophy.

CHAPTER 5

Samples, generalizations, and ideal types

Since the publication of the *Investigations*, Wittgenstein's ideas have exerted a great influence on the philosophy of the social sciences. Keynes was one of the first to feel this influence, and his use of the analysis of combinatory vagueness to defend the efficiency of ordinary language in formulating social theory is one of the most novel applications of Wittgenstein's philosophy. Keynes analysis of samples informed his views not only on the nature of concepts, but also his understanding of the nature of models in the social sciences. I now turn to look at why he believed models too were samples rather than generalizations.

Keynes often addressed the issue of why the social and natural sciences employ different methods. Many of the arguments he used in making this distinction are not novel, being similar to those pressed by philosophers of hermeneutics. He made much of the point, for example, that human action is meaningful and thus that social explanation requires an empathetic understanding of the thoughts and expectations of the social actors; and this requirement, he found, entailed his view on concept formation, for "as soon as one is dealing with the influence of expectations and of transitory experience, one is, in the nature of things, outside the realm of the formally exact."[1] He thus made a familiar hermeneutic case for conceptual adequacy. But what distinguishes his position from others is that he argued for this requirement largely on grounds of theoretical economy, and only in a cursory way on the basis of an ontological difference between nature and society. He also pressed a closely related argument to the hermeneutic one: like many philosophers of history he attached importance to "transitory experience," i.e. to the contingent features of a particular historical

[1] *Collected Works*, vol. 14, p. 2.

period in explaining the observed behavior of economies. This too is a familiar argument, bearing a resemblance to ones made by, amongst others, the neo-Kantians. But the analysis of combinatory vagueness and samples gives to his argument a surprising subtlety which allows him to skirt many of the pitfalls that have trapped other philosophers of hermeneutics.

HERMENEUTICS AND EXPECTATIONS

One of the features which distinguishes the social from the natural sciences is that human action, at least as seen as a social activity, is meaningful, it is done for reasons, it is actuated by beliefs about the future. To understand actions, then, we have to understand the reasons for their occurrence, and this means that the social sciences require an element of empathy with their subject-matter, they require what the neo-Kantians called *verstehen*. Philosophers of hermeneutics use this line of reasoning to argue that a purely behavioral social theory is either impossible, or at the least uninteresting. A social theory must be 'adequate' to its subject, it must be capable of being stated in terms which the subjects could understand, and with which they could identify. Peter Winch, in an influential Wittgensteinian interpretation of hermeneutics, argues that if this condition is not met the results of social theory will be as meaningful as an account of language that relies on "statistical laws about the likely occurrences of words."[2] This view implies that theorists draw upon the same tacit knowledge, the same common sense, as laymen do in the course of negotiating social life.

Keynes too argued for hermeneutic adequacy: when dealing with the fundamental assumptions of economic theory, he pointed out:

---

[2] *The Idea of a Social Science* (London: Routledge & Kegan Paul, 1958), p. 115. Winch's more Wittgensteinian understanding of meaningful behavior distinguishes him from previous philosophers of hermeneutics who had conceived of *verstehen* as a form of indwelling in the essentially private experiences of the agents under study. Drawing on Wittgenstein's demonstration of the untenability of a private, subjectivist account of meaning, Winch argues that meaningful behavior is rule-governed behavior, that rules are social phenomena, and therefore that grasping the meaning of a social action involves understanding the surrounding social context. This sociological activity he likened to philosophy itself, for grasping the meaning of an action involves the Wittgensteinian practice of excavating it from the social activities in which it is embedded.

The forces underlying and justifying these assumptions can only act by influencing the actions of individual businessmen. And we must justify our theoretical conclusions by displaying the individual motives which . . . bring about in the aggregate these theoretical conclusions . . . We must . . . make sure that we can *visualise* the forms in which they actually clothe themselves and through which they influence the minds of individuals.[3]

Keynes went to great efforts to maintain an immediately intelligible exposition, and to achieve adequacy by using concepts which the economic agents were themselves using. His belief in the greater efficiency of ordinary language in the social sciences was thus supported by a hermeneutic understanding of social theory. As was pointed out in the last chapter, his concepts were chosen, "so as to correspond to our actual psychology and ways of behaving and deciding and to enable us to answer the concrete questions which are likely to be asked":[4] Keynes's was "an analysis which is endeavouring to keep as close as it can to the actual facts of business calculation."[5] Thus, when working out his own definition of net income, for example, he argued that it will "not only come nearest to common usage," but that it also attains a *causal significance*" due to "the psychological influence . . . on the amount of current consumption, since *net income* is what we suppose the ordinary man to reckon his available income to be when he is deciding how much to spend on current consumption."[6] When considering Hayek's competing definition, as we have seen earlier, Keynes claimed that "no theoretical objection can be raised against [it] as providing a possible psychological criterion of net income" but merely stated that "I doubt if such an individual exists."[7] Keynes's approach did not preclude the use of terms which are not commonly found in business life; but he did imply that such unfamiliar terms must in principle be ones which economic agents could understand and identify with as being synonymous with ones they actually use. Winch makes this point about a Keynesian concept:

For example, liquidity preference is a technical concept of economics: it is not generally used by business men in the conduct of their affairs . . . But it is logically tied to concepts which do enter into business activity, for

---

[3] *Collected Works*, vol. 12, p. 731.
[4] *Collected Works*, vol. 13, p. 433.   [5] *Collected Works*, vol. 29, p. 88.
[6] *Collected Works*, vol. 7, p. 57.   [7] Ibid., p. 60.

its use by the economist presupposes his understanding of what it is to conduct a business.[8]

Similarly, when Keynes himself did adopt a definition that is not found in common usage, such as user cost, he was quick to add that "businessmen would seem to have the notion of user cost implicitly in mind, though they do not formulate it distinctly,"[9] indicating that he felt that the concept would be understood and accepted by economic agents.

Keynes drew a distinction between the natural and the social sciences when he argued "against Robbins, [that] economics is essentially a moral science, and not a natural science. That is to say, it employs introspection and judgments of value."[10] In other words, "it deals with motives, expectations, psychological uncertainties."[11] Intentionality entails another feature of the social world which distinguishes it from the mechanical world of physics, for, as Frank Knight put it, "an essential element in the phenomena is its lack of automatic mechanical accuracy, its liability to error."[12] Keynes thus cautioned:

One has to be constantly on guard against treating the material as constant and homogeneous. It is as though the fall of the apple to the ground depended on the apple's motives, on whether it is worth while falling to the ground, and whether the ground wanted the apple to fall, and on mistaken calculations on the part of the apple as to how far it was from the centre of the earth.[13]

---

[8] *The Idea of a Social Science*, p. 89. Alan Ryan also makes this point: "There can be no objection to concepts like that of the 'multiplier' or that of 'diminishing marginal utility'; for such concepts plainly get their meaning from what buyers and sellers themselves would say about their activities," *The Philosophy of the Social Sciences* (London: Macmillan, 1970), p. 153.
It should be noted, however, that the term "liquidity preference," at one time foreign to the ears of the business world, is now a familiar concept in the financial markets, and one which has passed into the common vocabulary of economic agents. This indicates a unique feature of the social sciences, i.e., the possibility of their explanations being adopted by the subjects they are studying, and even their ability to change the behavior of these subjects. Marxism and the theory of rational expectations embody an explicit recognition of this phenomenon. Antony Giddens refers to this feature as a "double hermeneutic": "there is continual 'slippage' of the concepts constructed in sociology, whereby these are appropriated by those whose conduct they were originally coined to analyse, and hence tend to become integral features *of* that conduct," *New Rules of Sociological Method* (New York: Basic Books, 1976), p. 162.

[9] *Collected Works*, vol. 7, p. 71.
[10] *Collected Works*, vol. 14, p. 297.   [11] Ibid., p. 300.
[12] *Risk, Uncertainty and Profit* (University of Chicago Press, 1971), p. 203.
[13] *Collected Works*, vol. 14, p. 300.

Intentionality was one reason Keynes gave for arguing that the social sciences must be methodologically different from the natural sciences.

It is dealt with most extensively in his analysis of expectations. Keynes took as the "independent variables" determining national income and employment, the wage-unit, the quantity of money, and the "three fundamental psychological factors, namely, the psychological propensity to consume, the psychological attitude to liquidity and the psychological expectation of future yield from capital-assets."[14] These factors of market psychology constitute our attitude towards the future, and because they are determined more by the expectation of future values than by current values monetary economies are unstable. Specifically, fluctuations in the marginal efficiency of capital are the cause of business cycles. When investors decide on the level of investment they must estimate the prospective yield of their assets over a period stretching further into the future than they are capable, with any certainty, of knowing.

> The outstanding fact is the extreme precariousness of the basis of knowledge on which our estimates of prospective yield have to be made. Our knowledge of the factors which will govern the yield of an investment some years hence is usually very slight and often negligible.[15]

In such conditions of uncertainty, in order to save "our faces as rational, economic men,"[16] we fall back on a series of conventions which consist, one, "in assuming that the existing state of affairs will continue indefinitely, except in so far as we have specific reasons to expect a change";[17] two, in assuming "that the *existing* state of opinion as expressed in prices . . . is based on a *correct* summing up of future prospects";[18] and three, in assuming that "the judgment of the rest of the world . . . is perhaps better informed."[19] As to whether or not these conventions save our faces as rational agents Keynes gave no clear answer. On the one hand he said that "It is reasonable . . . to be guided to a considerable degree by the facts about which we feel somewhat confident,"[20] these being the facts of the existing situation. His reasoning here follows from the distinction, drawn in his *Treatise on Probability*, between the

[14] *Collected Works*, vol. 7, pp. 246–7.
[15] Ibid., p. 149.   [16] *Collected Works*, vol. 14, p. 114.
[17] *Collected Works*, vol. 7, p. 152.   [18] *Collected Works*, vol. 14, p. 114.
[19] Ibid.   [20] *Collected Works*, vol. 7, p. 148.

probability of an argument and its weight.[21] The latter consideration concerns the absolute amount of information backing up an estimation of probability, and may be called the probability of the probability. So, in the case at hand, he suggested that it is rational to rely on the facts we know with most certainty because they carry the greatest weight. However, elsewhere he wrote, "The future never resembles the past – as we well know" and yet we "assume, contrary to all likelihood, that the future will resemble the past";[22] and further "we assume the future to be much more like the past than is reasonable."[23] And when, in the *Treatise on Probability* he considered the "reinsurance rates for the Waratah, a vessel which disappeared in South African waters,"[24] he clearly doubted the rationality of expectations:

The lapse of time made rates rise; the departure of ships in search of her made them fall; some nameless wreckage is found and they rise; it is remembered that in similar circumstances thirty years ago a vessel floated, helpless but not seriously damaged, for two months, and they fall. Can it be pretended that the figures which were quoted from day to day – 75 per cent, 83 per cent, 78 per cent – were rationally determinate, or that the actual figure was not within wide limits arbitrary and due to the caprice of individuals?[25]

At one point he combined both judgments in one sentence, suggesting that it is extremely difficult to define rational action under conditions of uncertainty:

the market will be subject to waves of optimistic and pessimistic sentiment, which are unreasoning and yet in a sense legitimate where no solid basis exists for a reasonable calculation.[26]

---

[21] *Collected Works*, vol. 8, ch. 6. For accounts which relate Keynes's treatment of expectations to his earlier work on probability, see Carabelli, *On Keynes's Method*, chs. 11–12; J. G. Meeks, "Keynes on the Rationality of Decision Procedures under Uncertainty: the Investment Decision," in *Thoughtful Economic Man. Essays on Rationality, Moral Rules and Benevolence*, edited by J. G. Meeks (Cambridge University Press, 1991), pp. 126–60; and R. M. O'Donnell, *Keynes: Philosophy, Economics and Politics* (New York: St. Martins Press, 1989).

[22] *Collected Works*, vol. 14, p. 124.

[23] Ibid., p. 125.

[24] *Collected Works*, vol. 8, pp. 24–5.

[25] Ibid.

[26] *Collected Works*, vol. 7, p. 154. J. G. Meeks, in "Keynes on the Rationality of Decision Procedures," compares the problem of analyzing rationality under conditions of uncertainty to the traditional philosophical problem of skepticism: in both cases we find ourselves in situations where rational grounds for our beliefs are lacking. Meeks argues that it is none the less possible to have reasonable beliefs.

Regardless of its rationality or otherwise, the important point about this form of knowledge is that, "being based on so flimsy a foundation, it is subject to sudden and violent changes."[27] When we accept a conventional valuation we recognize how little our judgment is based on, so "at all times the vague panic fears and equally vague and unreasoned hopes are not really lulled, and lie but a little way below the surface."[28] When a bit of "news" dampens our confidence or excites our expectations, and when once the convention begins to collapse, the process becomes cumulative and a bull or bear market is in the making. Thus one way in which uncertainty causes instability is through its effect on market sentiment. This is just one of two sources, for in addition to market speculation there is the influence of uncertainty on entrepreneurial activities:

Even apart from the instability due to speculation, there is the instability due to the characteristic of human nature that a large proportion of our positive activities depend on spontaneous optimism rather than on a mathematical expectation, whether moral or hedonistic or economic.[29]

Entrepreneurs are actuated in their enterprises by "animal spirits," and "a spontaneous urge to action rather than inaction,"[30] but the "delicate balance of spontaneous optimism" can be easily upset by the "news."[31] Keynes concluded that "It is not surprising that the volume of investment, thus determined, should fluctuate widely from time to time."[32] Given the importance of investment in aggregate demand, the analysis of investment is also "a theory of why output and employment are so liable to fluctuation."[33]

Keynes's use of the analysis of expectations and the argument for hermeneutics should be distinguished from that of other philosophers. Some have thought that a hermeneutic science has access to a realm of entities which are more familiar than any dealt with in the natural sciences; the natural world by contrast is silent and foreign to us, theory is underdetermined by nature. In the study of society, so the argument goes, we are, so to speak, studying our own kind and can therefore ask the subjects under study what they are doing. J. W. N. Watkins argues that Keynes believed in such a

---

[27] *Collected Works*, vol. 14, p. 114.
[28] Ibid., p. 115.   [29] *Collected Works*, vol 7, p. 161.
[30] Ibid., p. 161.   [31] Ibid., p. 162.
[32] *Collected Works*, vol. 14, p. 118.   [33] Ibid., p. 121.

privileged position for his theory because in the social sciences we are explaining "the familiar in terms of the familiar."[34] There is indeed something to the idea that common sense is isomorphic with the subject-matter of the social sciences. But the indeterminacy of translation makes nonsense out of the idea of cultural products being given to us in an unambiguous form. John Dunn nicely summarizes the main features of subjective experience which make hermeneutics considerably more complex than the more optimistic adherents, such as Dilthey, have thought:

Human mendacity and incompetence, technical problems in the theory of translation, the sparse and somewhat randomly selected records of states of consciousness which ever enter a public domain and the far sparser set of such records which remain at all durably within one[sic]. If what persons could have said under perfect interrogation forms the perfect text of human history [at the Last Judgement] what we can rationally and justifiably believe that they *did* say is likely to be a nastily mangled palimpsest.[35]

Similarly, Bernard Williams, drawing on the ideas of Quine and Davidson, argues for the "the conclusion that there are no fully determinate contents of the world which are its psychological contents."[36] Nor will Winch's recourse to the more public Wittgensteinian rules of usage save interpretive social science from the problem of indeterminacy, for any social action will correspond to many different rules.[37] Keynes, when earlier under the influence of Moore's form of phenomenology, did occasionally speak as if we could know the contents of consciousness in an unambiguous form. This belief however was always coupled with a candid appreciation of the complexity and organic nature of psychological phenomena. It was also a belief that he came to doubt, as we have seen. Furthermore, his account of expectations under conditions of uncertainty highlighted the extreme complexity and difficulty of social analysis, not its congeniality. The picture evoked by his account is one of a "kaleidic" economy, as G. L. S. Shackle has termed it, "a society interspersing its moments or intervals of

---

[34] "Ideal Types and Historical Explanation," in *The Philosophy of Social Explanation*, edited by Alan Ryan (Oxford University Press, 1973), pp. 95–6.
[35] "Practising History and Social Science on 'Realist' Assumptions," p. 88.
[36] *Descartes: The Project of Pure Inquiry* (Brighton: Harvester, 1979), p. 300.
[37] Hookway makes this point in "Indeterminacy and Interpretation," p. 39.

order, assurance and beauty with sudden disintegration and a cascade into a new pattern."[38]

The hermeneutic position also runs into problems when the requirement of conceptual adequacy is interpreted as a method-ological dictum. There is the implication here that all under-standing must be of the first-person variety; the third-person perspective is permitted only if it could in principle be translated into the first person. This is a difficult argument to maintain. As Rorty points out, "There are, after all, cases in which the other person's, or culture's, explanation of what it is up to is so primitive, or so nutty, that we brush it aside."[39] Hermeneutic adequacy does, however, retain its status as a "counsel of prudence," as Dunn calls it, for other reasons. It may save us a great deal of time in formulating theory: why start from scratch in concept formation if we can use the subject's own understanding as a first approxi-mation? And adequacy may be required if the questions we ask are couched in the terms used in social and political life, for then the answers, to be useful, should come back in the same language. But the third-person perspective cannot be ruled out as a conceptual impossibility. The most we can say is that a natural science of the social world may have little interest to us. This is apparent if we consider what use we would make of purely physical explanations of social phenomena. Hanna Pitkin questions the utility of this science:

a "purely observational" social science independent of our existing conceptual system in the realm of action might or might not be possible, might or might not be interesting or useful; but it could not tell us the things we now want to know about society and politics. It could not answer the questions we now can formulate, for they are formulated in the concepts we have.[40]

And John Dunn, while critical of hermeneutics for underestimating the difficulties stemming from translation, none the less points out:

Perhaps a *discreet* anti-hermeneutic human science could in principle even know the entire human future . . . [But] even a true science of human behaviour could not tell human action where it gets off. So far from being

---

[38] *Epistemics and Economics* (Cambridge University Press, 1972), p. 76.
[39] "Method, Social Science, and Social Hope," in *Consequences of Pragmatism* (Brighton: Harvester, 1982), p. 200.
[40] *Wittgenstein and Justice* (Berkeley: University of California Press, 1972), p. 274.

able in general simply to replace our own characterisations of our actions, an anti-hermeneutic human science can retain its epistemological respectability only by the consistent refusal to say anything about what we are *doing* and why we are doing it.[41]

Dunn adds "that no theory of human social action can be shown to be true in a rigidly anti-hermeneutic fashion."[42] Similarly, Rorty points out that 'value-free' social theories "will not be of much use unless they contain some of the terms which the policy-makers use among themselves."[43] Keynes also believed that a model in a policy science should be immediately significant, as he recommended that we "select those variables which can be deliberately controlled or managed by central authority in the kind of system in which we actually live."[44] It is difficult to know Keynes's views on issues in hermeneutics which have only subsequently emerged. But it is clear from his comments on the choice of language for his theory that economy of expression was a guiding concern. And this, as we have seen, he believed was served by conceptual adequacy.

IDEAL TYPES

The difficulties expectations present for model building are matched by those entailed by Keynes's view that it is the historically specific features of society that must be understood in order to answer many of the questions asked in the social sciences, and in macro-economics in particular. This is another view he shared with the neo-Kantians. Keynes, like Max Weber before him, thought it was the particular and transitory psychologies and institutions of society that are of interest in a policy science such as economics. And these Keynes thought "non-homogeneous through time":[45] institutions, expectations, and behavioral propensities are constantly changing, yet we must use them as causal factors in explaining the observed behavior of an economy. He made this point when praising Malthus for "taking up the tale much nearer its conclusion," than Ricardo's more mechanistic theory had.[46]

---

[41] "Practising History and Social Science on 'Realist' Assumptions," p. 86.
[42] Ibid., p. 87.   [43] "Method, Social Science, and Social Hope," p. 196.
[44] *Collected Works*, vol. 7, p. 247.
[45] *Collected Works*, vol. 14, p. 286.   [46] *Collected Works*, vol. 10, p. 88.

Malthus dwelled on the level of the particular, and Keynes quoted him on this approvingly:

I certainly am disposed to refer frequently to things as they are, as the only way of making one's writings practically useful to society, and I think also the only way of being secure from falling into the errors of the taylors of Laputa, and by a slight mistake at the outset arrive at conclusions the most distant from the truth. Besides I really think that the progress of society consists of irregular movements, and that to omit the consideration of causes which for eight or ten years will give a great *stimulus* to production and population, or a great *check* to them, is to omit the causes of the wealth and poverty of nations.[47]

Much of the debate on method in the social sciences might be reinterpreted in light of this philosophical discussion of knowledge interests and levels of reality. There is an entire spectrum of perspectives varying in their relative interest in the universal or particular features of phenomena. It is a spectrum running from the abstract to the concrete. Thus, physics abstracts from all particularity and looks at the universal properties all matter shares; psychology brings in more of the specifically human; history and politics bring in more of the social institutions; and in our personal lives it is, so to speak, the complete individual that is considered. The peculiar position the social sciences find themselves in is that they have not yet agreed on where on the spectrum they belong. Behaviorists have tried to settle next door to physics. Keynes on the other hand placed the moral sciences, or macro-economics at any rate, closer to the concrete end. For him it was the particular and transitory psychologies and institutions of an economy that are of interest in a policy science such as economics. Of course, where on the spectrum the social sciences belong is not the sort of issue that can be settled once and for all, as the position will vary depending on the sort of question being asked. Indeed, part of the problem of the philosophy of the social sciences may stem from the attempt to locate our place on this spectrum once and for all, independently of the issue under discussion.

Keynes's more historical understanding of society however raises the problem of how to think systematically about a particular historical period. The German Historical School of economics had shared with Keynes an appreciation of the importance of

[47] Ibid., pp. 97–8.

contingencies in understanding society, but had done so at the cost of foregoing theory almost completely. Keynes thought this a mistake and addressed the Historical School in the preface to the German edition of the *General Theory*:

It can scarcely be claimed, however, that this school of thought has erected a rival theoretical construction; or has even attempted to do so. It has been sceptical, realistic, content with historical and empirical methods and results, which discard formal analysis . . . Thus Germany, quite contrary to her habit in most of the sciences, has been content for a whole century to do without any formal theory of economics.[48]

Keynes hoped that his theory would fill this gap in German economics.

Keynes's proposed solution to the ongoing Methodenstreit in both Germany and England was again similar to that of Weber. Although Keynes does not use the term, his comments on the nature of models in the social sciences show that he employed what Weber called "ideal types." These are thinking models, systematic representations of the characteristic features of a historical situation. As Weber said, "In its conceptual purity, this mental construct . . . cannot be found empirically anywhere in reality. It is a *utopia*."[49] Keynes too believed that the purpose of a model

is to segregate the semi-permanent or relatively constant factors from those which are transitory or fluctuating so as to develop a logical way of thinking about the latter, and of understanding the time sequences to which they give rise in particular cases.[50]

And just as Weber said that ideal types "are meant to *approximate*" the historical reality being studied by "unifying those properties which we regard as *'characteristic,'*"[51] so too Keynes said that the economist "selects . . . a fairly typical case out of the genus which he is in fact discussing, and talks in terms of this."[52] The notion of an ideal type gives us another light under which to read Keynes's

---

[48] *Collected Works*, vol. 7, pp. xxv–xxvi.

[49] *The Methodology of the Social Sciences*, translated and edited by E. Shils and H. Finch (Glencoe: Free Press, 1949), p. 90. For a good survey of Weber's approach to concept formation, as well as those of Rickert and Dilthey, see Thomas Burger, *Max Weber's Theory of Concept Formation* (Durham: Duke University Press, 1976).

[50] *Collected Works*, vol. 14, pp. 296–7.

[51] *Roscher and Knies: The Logical Problems of Historical Economics*, translated by Guy Oakes (New York: Free Press, 1975), p. 57.

[52] *Collected Works*, vol. 29, p. 36.

comments, previously quoted that models are "a sample statement, so to speak, out of all the things which could be said,"[53] and "a generalisation which lacks precise statement of the cases to which the generalisation applies."[54]

Since the features chosen for inclusion in an ideal type will depend on the question being asked, there are, as Weber said, "a very great many utopias of capitalism."[55] The decision of what part of concrete reality to incorporate into a model, both Keynes and Weber termed a "value judgment." Keynes wrote

When one is separating for purposes of analysis elements which are seldom or never discoverable in isolation in the real world, there is an arbitrary element, and one must be governed by what seems most instructive and helpful in understanding the substantial issue.[56]

Furthermore, the "substantial issue" will change with history; institutions and beliefs change and with them the questions we wish to answer. Thus, an economist, Keynes said, "does not require a highly specialised intellectual technique," as is found in the hard sciences; he "must contemplate the particular in terms of the general, and touch abstract and concrete in the same flight of thought.[57] These are requisite qualities because an economist's task is the selection, manipulation, and application of ideal types to changing economic conditions:

Economics is a science of thinking in terms of models joined to the art of choosing models which are relevant to the contemporary world. It is compelled to be this, because, unlike the typical natural science, the material to which it is applied is, in too many respects, not homogeneous through time.[58]

Models for Keynes derived their "usefulness [from being] an instrument of thought";[59] and thus "the habit of mind which is most important for an economist to acquire" is "the art of thinking in terms of models."[60] Keynes pointed out that this is "a difficult – largely because it is an unaccustomed – practice," and recognized the prevalent tendency to try to convert economics into a "pseudo-natural-science,"[61] In his discussion of econometrics he made the following distinction: in the natural sciences

[53] *Collected Works*, vol. 13, p. 470.   [54] *Collected Works*, vol 29, p. 38.
[55] *Methodology of the Social Sciences*, p. 91.   [56] *Collected Works*, vol. 29, p. 265.
[57] *Collected Works*, vol. 10, p. 141.   [58] *Collected Works*, vol. 14, p. 296.
[59] Ibid., vol. 14, p. 299.   [60] Ibid., p. 300.   [61] Ibid., p. 296.

the object of experiment is to fill in the actual values of the various quantities and factors appearing in an equation or a formula; and the work when done is once and for all. In economics that is not the case, and to convert a model into a quantitative formula is to destroy its usefulness as an instrument of thought.[62]

If coefficients are specified "the model loses its generality and its value as a model of thought."[63] Keynes thought his own *General Theory* provided just such a model, one that accounted for "the outstanding characteristics of the economic system in which we live."[64] Yet he never accorded it the status of being "a machine, or method of blind manipulation";[65] it was a significant theoretical construct for the understanding of a specific historical configuration. After outlining the factors he found significant for his model he nicely summarizes the nature and purpose of ideal types:

there is not one of the above factors which is not liable to change without much warning, and sometimes substantially. Hence the extreme complexity of the actual course of events. Nevertheless, these seem to be the factors which it is useful and convenient to isolate. If we examine any actual problem along the lines of the above schematism, we shall find it more manageable; and our practical intuition (which can take account of a more detailed complex of facts than can be treated on general principles) will be offered a less intractable material upon which to work.[66]

The complexity of historical phenomena as well as the chaotic behavior of expectations led Keynes to believe that in the social sciences we are "outside the realm of the formally exact." These aspects of economic and historical reality are more efficiently handled by the concepts of ordinary language.

Keynes's view that the questions we ask of society are historically conditioned and therefore that the features of society which interest us are historically specific has been dealt with by a number of philosophers since his day. Nelson Goodman, for one, argues for an ontology that recognizes any world that corresponds to our interests; there are therefore an indefinite number of worlds. Physical, chemical, and biological accounts of, say, a plant, all reveal different realities of the object. So too does our aesthetic appreciation of the object; and here each artistic rendering of it will reveal

[62] Ibid., p. 299.   [63] Ibid., p. 296.
[64] *Collected Works*, vol. 7, p. 249.
[65] Ibid., p. 297.   [66] Ibid., p. 249.

a separate reality.[67] Goodman disagrees with Quine in that he sees no reason for according the physical account any priority. A similar case is made by Michael Polanyi. He calls all these perspectives "levels of reality," and in his philosophical work, *Personal Knowledge*, demonstrates that they cannot be reduced one to another. His specific target of attack was what he called "objectivism." a doctrine similar to Quine's physicalism. This is the attempt to gain access to the fundamental layer of reality by reducing "all knowledge to strictly impersonal terms," such as those of physics.[68] He sets out instead to demonstrate all the types of "personal knowledge" required in each science. For example, one might think that the reality of a machine is grasped only by physics, for after all a machine is "objectively" only a hunk of matter, an inanimate object. However:

A physical and chemical investigation cannot convey the understanding of a machine as expressed by its operational principles. In fact, it can say nothing at all about the way the machine works or ought to work.[69]

And if it is knowledge about a machine that we want, this form of reductive analysis can tell us almost nothing: "*The complete knowledge of a machine as an object tells us nothing about it as a machine.*"[70] What is required for machine-knowledge is the more personal knowledge of human contrivance. Polanyi goes on to apply the same anti-objectivist argument to show how the various different biological and human sciences are irreducible to the more impersonal and supposedly objective ones. He sketches out the "ascending stages of biological knowledge," and shows that at each stage an additional element of empathy or personal knowledge is required.[71]

The same point about multiple realities is made by several social theorists. Alfred Schutz, founder of phenomenological sociology, talks of "provinces of meaning,"[72] each of which varies depending on the degree of intimacy and anonymity: the better we know someone or some social group the less are we interested in their

67 See *Ways of Worldmaking* (Indianapolis: Hackett, 1978).
68 *Personal Knowledge. Towards a Post-Critical Philosophy* (University of Chicago Press, 1958), p. 329.
69 Ibid.   70 Ibid., p. 330.
71 Ibid., p. 364.
72 *Collected Papers*, vol. 1, edited by Maurice Natanson (The Hague: Martinus Nijhoff, 1964), p. 230.

generic properties and more in their individuality. We can focus on man's universal properties, as is done in medicine, for people at all times share some bodily functions; in this respect all people are the same. But that perspective declines in importance as we ascend into more personal realms: in politics all people are not the same (Hitler is different to Ghandi); nor are they in their love lives (This is the person I love, and none other will do). Schutz's main concern is with the "life world," and the spectrum of interests he concentrates on continues for the social world what Polanyi has analyzed in the biological world.[73] In the social sciences our knowledge is more personal because more concrete. Now in all these examples from Goodman, Polanyi, and Schutz, it may be possible to carry out the reduction to an impersonal level: a machine can be seen as a hunk of metal, a dog as a bundle of sense data, a close friend as a complicated group of cells, but to do so destroys the type of knowledge that we were interested in in the first place – knowledge of a machine, an animal, a friend. In short, we have a wide range of knowledge interests, and corresponding to each a type of knowledge, a level of reality, that is not reducible to a lower level without losing its original meaning.

The issue of significance, or levels of interest, was also discussed in later Cambridge philosophy. Russell, for example, being Quine's philosophical ancestor, was critical of hermeneutic psychology, and was a qualified adherent of behaviorism, the gist of which he took to be "that in psychology we are to rely wholly upon external observations and never to accept data for which the evidence is entirely derived from introspection."[74] This is the opposite position to that taken by Keynes. In addition to Russell's expressed preference for a scientific psychology, he also recounted that "along with the prejudice in favour of behaviourist methods there went another prejudice in favour of explanation in terms of physics wherever possible."[75] In confessing this prejudice he is explicit in identifying his relative lack of interest in the more personal and particular realms of knowledge:

---

[73] Polanyi also analyses the human sciences. See *The Study of Man* (University of Chicago Press, 1959). Raymond Aron compares Polanyi's anti-objectivism with that of Weber in "Max Weber and Michael Polanyi," *The Logic of Personal Knowledge. Essays Presented to Michael Polanyi on His Seventieth Birthday, 11th March, 1961* (London: Routledge & Kegan Paul, 1961).

[74] *My Philosophical Development*, p. 96.   [75] Ibid.

I have always been deeply persuaded that, from a cosmic point of view, life and experience are causally of little importance. The world of astronomy dominates my imagination and I am very conscious of the minuteness of our planet in comparison with the systems of galaxies.[76]

Ramsey expressed an interest in quite the opposite side of reality in a passage Keynes included in his anthology, and one Russell quoted as "expressing what I do *not* feel":

My picture of the world is drawn in perspective, and not like a model to scale. The foreground is occupied by human beings and the stars are all as small as threepenny bits . . . I apply my perspective not merely to space but also to time. In time the world will cool and everything will die; but that is a long time off still, and its present value at compound discount is almost nothing. Nor is the present less valuable because the future will be blank. Humanity, which fills the foreground of my picture, I find interesting and on the whole admirable.[77]

The issue of significance was not central to the transition in Cambridge philosophy, but it is no coincidence that views on the reductive project of analytic philosophy should coincide with these more casual comments on each philosopher's interests.

A CAMBRIDGE METHOD

Keynes thus held similar views on the nature of model building to those of the Neo-Kantians. He may well have felt the influence of this school through the teaching of his mentor, Alfred Marshall, who spent time in Germany and was himself influenced by the more historical bias of economics there. I do not know if this was how Keynes inherited his views. However, there was a precedent within Cambridge for the use of such thinking models. K. T. Fann has argued that both Sraffa and Wittgenstein manipulated simplified, characteristic scenarios as a way of analyzing complex phenomena. He also suggests that Wittgenstein may have picked up this approach from Sraffa in the course of their discussions during the early thirties. Fann, in attempting to piece together this influence, pointed out that Sraffa and Wittgenstein used "the method of speculative anthropology."[78] Wittgenstein would imagine simplified language games, and from these scenarios he

---

[76] Ibid.   [77] Ibid., pp. 96–7. Also in Keynes, *Collected Works*, vol. 10, p. 345.
[78] *Wittgenstein's Conception of Philosophy*, p. 49.

would piece together the more complex meanings of words. The *Investigations*, and indeed all his later work, is filled with passages such as "Imagine a language-game in which A asks and B reports the number of slabs or blocks in a pile, or the colours and shapes of the building-stones that are stacked in such-and-such a place."[79] Fann's point is that this practice of imagining simplified societies is similar to the method used by Sraffa in *Production of Commodities by Means of Commodities*. The book begins "Let us consider an extremely simple society which produces just enough to maintain itself."[80] And, as Fann points out, the book continues on and "builds up the more complicated forms by gradually adding new features."[81] Alessandro Roncaglia has also recognized the similarity between the two thinkers' methodology, and he adds that another important point of agreement is the understanding that these simple linguistic or economic activities are not necessarily reducible one to another; they do not point to necessary and sufficient conditions which must be present for meaning or economic exchange to be identified.[82]

This Wittgensteinian/Sraffian method is similar to that of ideal types in that simplified scenarios are used to analyze, or highlight, certain characteristic relations within a more complex structure, but without purporting to be generalizations. Wittgenstein wrote:

Our clear and simple language-games are not preparatory studies for a future regularization of language – as it were first approximations, ignoring friction and air-resistance. The language-games are rather set up as *objects of comparison* which are meant to throw light on the facts of our language by way not only of similarities, but also of dissimilarities.[83]

And further:

we can avoid ineptness or emptiness in our assertions only by presenting the model as what it is, as an object of comparison – as, so to speak, a measuring-rod; not as a preconceived idea to which reality *must* correspond.[84]

Keynes indeed interpreted his own model along lines similar to these: his "schematism" or "sample statement" was intended more

---

[79] *Investigations*, sect. 21.　　[80] (Cambridge University Press, 1960), p. 3.

[81] *Wittgenstein's Conception of Philosophy*, p. 49.

[82] *Sraffa and the Theory of Prices*, translated by J. A. Kregel (Chichester: John Wiley, 1978), p. 123.

[83] *Investigations*, sect. 130.　　[84] Ibid., sect. 131.

as a heuristic device to help both the economist and reader, and not as an empirically testable generalization. Keynes thus shared this methodological view with his Cambridge colleagues.

The similarities between the models used by Keynes, Wittgenstein, and Sraffa can also be seen as stemming from the discovery at that time of the importance of combinatory vagueness. If entities falling under the application of a term need share few if any common features then the nature of definition becomes problematic. In this situation a definition cannot specify a common property, it cannot be a generalization; it can only describe a sample. Wittgenstein did not spend much time analyzing the nature of definition, just its absence from natural language. However, in the later development of his thought by cognitive psychologists and theorists of fuzzy logic more attention has been paid to the summarizing role played by our concepts. We may know implicitly how to apply our concepts to myriad objects, but to simplify the task of thought and speech we employ what have been called "prototypes'," i.e. paradigm objects that are recognized as indisputable samples of the term.[85] The sample chosen, however, need not share certain core properties with all the objects referred to by the term; it is just the sample that summarizes the most information. I think Keynes's views on concept formation were informed by similar thoughts. Just as Wittgenstein had maintained that definition appears long after we can use our words – "We talk, we utter words, and only *later* get a picture of their life."[86] – so too Keynes had pointed out to his students that "You can think accurately and effectively long before you can, so to speak, photograph your thought."[87] In his lectures of 1933 he discussed the use of paradigms:

A generalisation to cover everything is impossible and impracticable. Generalising in economics is thinking by sample, not by generalisation. There is no possible use of mechanical logic, you only have it for a sample case not a general case.[88]

[85] This problem of definition resembles somewhat the difficulty Kant encountered when he tried to account for the way schematized categories effect their mediation between the pure categories and the sensuous manifold. Prototypes and Kant's schematized categories could be fruitfully compared. It is interesting in this connection, although probably only a coincidence, that Keynes termed the constructs he used to order the chaos of social reality "schematisms." See for example *Collected Works*, vol. 7, p. 249.
[86] *Investigations*, p. 209.
[87] Rymes, *Keynes's Lectures*, p. 102.   [88] Ibid., p. 101.

Thus the task at hand is the choice of samples that highlight the important phenomena for the question being asked. "In economics one's thinking is perforce not truly by generalisations but rather by sample. You must always see whether the imperfections in your sample case are relevant or irrelevant to your conclusion."[89] The simplified scenarios used by Keynes, Wittgenstein, and Sraffa, indeed ideal types themselves, can thus be fruitfully interpreted as prototypes for analyzing complex social phenomena. I return to this issue in the concluding chapter.

The chain of influence suggested above can also throw light on some related comments of Keynes's, these being his remarks that economics is "a moral science"[90] and "a branch of logic."[91] Both of these comments can be interpreted in a fairly straightforward manner, without reference to later Cambridge philosophy: Keynes meant by moral sciences merely those disciplines which deal with humans in their social existence. And by calling economics a branch of logic he was using the phrase in the same sense as he and Moore did when they subsumed ethics under the umbrella of logic. This is admittedly an unusually wide conception of logic, as the study of ethical notions is not normally included in a field commonly confined to the study of valid inference. Keynes, by including ethics as a branch of logic, obviously had a wider conception of logic. He does not make this wider sense of the term clear, but I think it can be surmised that, as part of his and Moore's earlier phenomeno-logical projects, logic included the study of entities which are purely ideational, entities, that is, which can only be grasped by attending to the contents of consciousness, and not through an empirical analysis of natural objects. Ethics was considered a branch of logic because the meaning of its central concepts could not be found through a scientific treatment, but only by attending to the unanalyzable givens of consciousness. Thus, logic would include the timeless and phenomenological laws of demonstration, the rela-tions of probable knowledge, or so Keynes thought, and the notions of ethics, which, it will be remembered, were not under-stood as naturalistic entities. Keynes abandoned much of this early phenomenology, but there is a thread of continuity here with his later views. After sketching out Keynes's use of ideal types, or

[89] Ibid., p. 102.
[90] *Collected Works*, vol. 14, p. 297.   [91] Ibid., p. 296.

his thinking models, and the complicated non-representational relation they bore to reality, it is possible to see that Keynes thought economics too was "a branch of logic" because it is, in his words, "a way of thinking,"[92] it involved manipulating mental constructions, "model[s] of thought,"[93] ones that were not merely empirical representations. Within later Cambridge philosophy these comments may have gained an added meaning with the development of Wittgenstein's ideas. There is a passage in the *Investigations* which indicates that a slight extension of the meaning of the words "logic" and "normative science" may have occurred in the Cambridge philosophical community. Wittgenstein reported:

F. P. Ramsey once emphasized in conversation with me that logic was a "normative science." I do not know exactly what he had in mind, but it was doubtless closely related to what only dawned on me later: namely, that in philosophy we often compare the use of words with games and calculi which have fixed rules, but cannot say that someone who is using language must be playing such a game . . . [L]ogic does not treat of language – or of thought – in the sense in which a natural science treats of a natural phenomenon, and the most that can be said is that we *construct* ideal languages. But here the word "ideal" is liable to mislead, for it sounds as if these languages were better, more perfect, than our everyday language.[94]

Within the later Cambridge philosophical scene the terms "logic" and "moral" or "normative science" may have been used in an idiosyncratic way; and Keynes, being part of this community, may have come to use these terms in a similar manner when he penned his comments on economic models. Wittgenstein's description of the normative function of logic indeed sounds similar to many of Keynes's comments concerning the role of "value judgments" in the construction of ideal types and in the comparison of these with economic reality, i.e., in "the art of choosing models which are relevant to the contemporary world."[95] Both thinkers employed "ideal" constructs in their studies, by which they meant that the model being employed does not strictly represent empirical reality, or does not emerge out of empirical study in the manner of a theory in the natural sciences; it is an invention, a sample, one of an indefinite number of possible models, designed

---

[92] Ibid.   [93] Ibid.
[94] *Investigations*, sect. 81.   [95] *Collected Works*, vol. 14, p. 296.

for highlighting a specific aspect of reality. Keynes's models thus exemplify a form of ideal type construction that Wittgenstein and Ramsey also employed when trying to make sense out of the welter of language games. Keynes was I believe the first to apply the work done within linguistic philosophy on combinatorial vagueness and samples to the problem of model building in the social sciences.

CHAPTER 6

The Cambridge philosophical community

The similarities between Keynes's and Wittgenstein's later views on language and vagueness are striking. The textual comparison of the previous chapters thus helps explain many of Keynes's unorthodox preferences in model building. But the influence of Wittgenstein on Keynes has been doubted by some biographers, and largely ignored by others. However, I do not believe the whole story has been told of Keynes's friendship with Wittgenstein in particular, and his involvement with later Cambridge philosophy generally. When this story is sketched in we can see that Keynes was following the new philosophical ideas more closely than has been appreciated.

In the existing literature on Keynes it is often argued that his views on method and the general outlines of his philosophical position were set in the early twenties, at the time of his *Treatise on Probability*. Anna Carabelli, for example, argues that "Keynes's own economic methodology had its roots in that early work" and that "on this aspect [he] seemed not to have changed his mind."[1] Furthermore, in the historical and biographical work on Cambridge philosophy there has been very little written specifically on Keynes's friendships with Ramsey and Wittgenstein, and more generally on the fruitful collaboration between the economists and the philosophers. And what little has been written underestimates Keynes's involvement with the later philosophical ideas. Ray Monk claims that Wittgenstein's friendship with Keynes was confined to purely practical affairs shortly after his return to Cambridge in 1929,[2] that there was little intellectual rapport between the two,

---

[1] *On Keynes's Method*, pp. 7–8. Similar arguments are developed in Donald Moggridge, *Keynes* (London: MacMillan, 1976), and O'Donnell, *Keynes: Philosophy, Economics and Politics*.

[2] *Ludwig Wittgenstein. The Duty of Genius* (Harmondsworth: Penguin, 1990), p. 261.

that Wittgenstein even had a low opinion of Keynes's under-standing of philosophy.[3] These claims, of course, are not incon-sistent with the possibility that Keynes was greatly influenced by Wittgenstein. One need not be a friend, nor even have a deep understanding, of a philosopher in order to be influenced by his ideas. After all, Wittgenstein had few close friends, and he despaired of anyone understanding the *Investigations*. He was none the less extremely influential. The textual evidence so far considered certainly supports the claim that this influence extended to Keynes. And this is a possibility that is not explored by current accounts of his philosophy.

The work so far on Keynes's philosophy, and on his comments on method in the social sciences, looks back to its roots in the early stages of analytic philosophy; and the bulk of commentary focuses on the *Treatise on Probability* and on the influence of Moore's *Principia Ethica*. The trouble with confining one's attention to these years is that the bulk of Keynes's notes on the philosophy of the social sciences was written during the thirties, a period during which Cambridge philosophy was in the midst of an intellectual revolution – it was questioning most of the tenets of analytic philosophy. So it could be quite misleading to interpret a Cambridge philosopher only in terms of his early work. It would be analogous to interpreting the *General Theory* in terms of the *Treatise on Money* or, earlier, the *Tract on Monetary Reform*. Such an exercise can be helpful in charting a thinker's development, in finding early traces of a later doctrine, but it is not sufficient for under-standing new ideas. Besides, one can find traces of many different lines of thought in the early Keynes: if he had turned out to be a monetarist, to employ the *reductio ad absurdum*, one could find plenty of evidence for his early adherence to the Quantity Theory.[4]

Another problem with arguing for the predominant influence of the *Treatise on Probability* on Keynes's later thought is that after 1930

---

[3] Ibid., p. 414.
[4] Although see Allan Meltzer's case for thinking Keynes believed in a 'monetary rule'. "Keynes' General Theory: A Different Perspective," *Journal of Economic Literature* 19 (March 1981), pp. 34–64; and in *Keynes and the Modern World*, edited by James Trevithick and David Worswick (Cambridge University Press, 1983), p. 69, n. 31. C. A. E. Goodhart takes him to task on this in the Trevithick and Worswick volume, p. 76.

he ceased to write on the subject.[5] There is just too little textual evidence at hand to argue for his continuing involvement with issues in probability. The philosophical beliefs which informed the method of the *General Theory* are contained rather in the manuscripts, letters, and lecture notes considered in the past few chapters. These all date from the thirties, and deal with issues, such as vagueness, that were only tangentially mentioned, if at all, before. It is the philosophical reasoning behind these passages that has needed interpretation. For it is within the context of later Cambridge philosophy, rather than the context of early analytic philosophy, that Keynes's mature position on the language of social explanation can find its home context. It is also there that we find some sort of defense against the claims that it is, in one critic's words, "slack and intellectually lazy *obiter dicta*,"[6] or, according to another, "emotional utterances."[7] Collecting his later writings on philosophical subjects shows that the issues he considered important were ones that were then being debated in Cambridge. Keynes along with the other philosophers had moved on to a new analysis of language, one that highlighted its discontinuity with formal logic rather than its affinity. This move beyond the logical analyses of analytic philosophy and away from Moore's phenomenology is suggested in Keynes's later essay "My Early Beliefs," where he wrote of the "thin rationalism" of his pre-War colleagues.[8] What has been largely missing from the literature are the philosophical details of this transition, something I hope now to have provided, and the biographical details of Keynes's friendships with the philosophers that would account for his knowledge of later Cambridge philosophy, something I turn to in this chapter.

Setting out the details of Keynes's personal relationships with the Cambridge philosophers is thus, at the least, an interesting chapter in their biographies which needs to be written. For the

[5] Skidelsky considers Keynes's diminished interest in probability during this period and casually concludes that "It may be that nothing much needs to be said about this beyond the fact that Keynes's attention had shifted," *Keynes. The Economist as Saviour*, p. 87.

[6] Frank Hahn, *In Praise of Economic Theory*, The Jevons Memorial Fund Lecture, University College (London: University College, 1984), p. 18.

[7] Richard Stone, "Keynes, Political Arithmetic and Econometrics," from the *Proceedings of the British Academy*, 64 (Oxford University Press, 1978), p. 60.

[8] *Collected Works*, vol. 10, p. 450.

Cambridge philosophical community included several economists. Keynes and Frank Ramsey published important works in both economics and philosophy.[9] And they, together with Sraffa, were, during this period, good friends with Wittgenstein, Moore, and Russell; they were intimately involved with the debates within analytic philosophy; and all three were involved in criticizing the ideas, or proof-reading the manuscripts, which eventually issued in Wittgenstein's *Investigations*. The philosophers and economists thus formed a relatively tight-knit group of thinkers, with cross-references and acknowledgements cropping up in all their work. But the biographical story also enables me to move beyond a case relying on textual similarities to making a case of influence. The possibility of Keynes being influenced by the debates surrounding the *Investigations* is one, as I have pointed out, which has been denied. However, it is *prima facie* unlikely that Keynes would have come away from discussions with his philosopher friends during those tempestuous times without absorbing at least some of the new ideas. He was, after all, a philosopher, and the development of the *Investigations* was one of the major events of twentieth-century philosophy. So there is an interesting story here that fills in a missing piece in the story of Cambridge philosophy, i.e. Keynes's position in the Cambridge philosophical community during the thirties. This is missing in the literature both on Keynes and on Cambridge philosophy.

WITTGENSTEIN

Keynes and Wittgenstein became close friends from the time they first met, in October 1912. Shortly after their meeting, Keynes wrote to Duncan Grant:

Wittgenstein is a most wonderful character – what I said about him when I saw you last is quite untrue – and extraordinarily nice. I like enormously to be with him.[10]

Keynes recognized Wittgenstein's genius from the start, and subsequently made great efforts to facilitate Wittgenstein's work.

---

[9] Ramsey's articles were "A Contribution to the Theory of Taxation," *The Economic Journal* 37 (1927), pp. 47–61; and "A Mathematical Theory of Saving", *The Economic Journal* 38 (1928), pp. 543–9.

[10] Letter of November 12, 1912. Quoted in Harrod, *Keynes*, p. 161.

In Harrod's assessment, even though "a great friendship eventually sprang up with Russell . . . the friendship with Keynes was in some ways more important."[11] Keynes, he continued, was "able to have some influence on Wittgenstein in his practical life, and he was always his advocate."[12] Shortly after their meeting, Keynes helped get Wittgenstein elected to the Apostles, despite Russell's opposition.[13] Later, Keynes was to lend Wittgenstein money on several occasions;[14] and he used his influence in diplomatic circles to facilitate Wittgenstein's dream of visiting Russia.

In addition, the two followed each others progress by exchanging books and manuscripts. Keynes's influence at the Foreign Office was instrumental in getting the manuscript of the *Tractatus* sent to England from a prison-camp in Italy, where Wittgenstein was held after Austria surrendered in 1918. In a letter from Monte Cassino, dated 12.6.19, Wittgenstein informed Russell, "Some days ago I sent you my manuscript, through Keynes's good offices."[15] And to Keynes he wrote "have you done any more work on probability? My M-S. contains a few lines about it which, I believe, – solve the essential question."[16] Later, in 1923–4, Keynes read the book, and in answer to Wittgenstein's query sent him his latest publications:

I have sent you in a separate package copies of the various books which I have written since the war. *Probability* is the completion of what I was doing before the war – I fear you will not like it. Two books on the Peace Treaty, half economic half political, a book on Monetary Reform . . . [17]

---

[11] Harrod, *Keynes*, p. 161.

[12] Ibid.

[13] For the story of Wittgenstein's election to the Apostles, and Keynes's participation, see Paul Levy, *Moore: G. E. Moore and the Cambridge Apostles* (Oxford University Press, 1979), pp. 266–70; Skidelsky, *Keynes: Hopes Betrayed*, p. 266.

[14] Keynes's loans usually led to misunderstanding. In May, 1929 Wittgenstein wrote to Keynes, embarrassed by what he thought was "an undertone of grudge" on Keynes's side: "I thought probably you think that I cultivate your friendship amongst other reasons to be able get some financial assistance from you," Wittgenstein, *Letters to Russell, Keynes and Moore*, edited by G. H. von Wright (Oxford: Basil Blackwell, 1974), p. 128. Keynes replied: "What a maniac you are! Of course there is not a particle of truth in anything you say about money," May 26, 1929, ibid., p. 129.

[15] In Bertrand Russell, *Autobiography. Vol. II: 1915–44* (London: Routledge & Kegan Paul, 1967), p. 117.

[16] Wittgenstein, *Letters to Russell, Keynes, and Moore*, dated 12/6/19, p. 112.

[17] Ibid., dated March 29, 1924, p. 116. Earlier Keynes had also sent Wittgenstein an article he had written for the *Manchester Guardian*: Wittgenstein responded "Thanks so much for sending me the Reconstruction in Europe," ibid., dated 1923, p. 113.

The exchange, however, was not fruitful, for Keynes, after apologizing for not writing earlier, wrote:

The reason was that I wanted to try to understand your book thoroughly before writing to you; yet my mind is now so far from fundamental questions that it is impossible for me to get clear about such matters. I still do not know what to say about your book, except that I feel certain that it is a work of extraordinary importance and genius. Right or wrong, it dominates all fundamental discussions at Cambridge since it was written.[18]

On Wittgenstein's side the response to the *Treatise on Probability* was much the same:

Since I'm very busy and my brain is quite incapable of absorbing anything of a scientific character I've only read parts of *one* of the books ["The economic consequences of the Peace"]. It interested me very much, though of course I understand practically nothing about the subject.[19]

Wittgenstein did, however, appreciate Keynes's book *A short View of Russia*: "About your book I forgot to say that I liked it. It shows that you know that there are more things between heaven and earth etc." [20]

At this stage then, during the early 1920s, there is little evidence of any direct influence one way or the other, and little even to suggest that they were thinking along similar lines. Keynes indicated as much in a letter of 11/15/25 to his wife, Lydia: "Last night I tried to explain the philosophy of Ludwig to my Society: but it escapes the mind – I could only half remember it."[21] Keynes did feel it was important to encourage Wittgenstein's philosophising: "I would do anything in my power which could make it easier for you to do further work."[22] But he also indicated some areas of disagreement: in the letter just quoted, he says of the *Treatise* "I fear you will not like it"; and later he was to refer to the "obscure contents" of the *Tractatus*[23]. Finally, as Robert Skidelsky points out, "Wittgenstein was fundamentally opposed to the view of ethics as a

---

[18] Ibid., dated March 29, 1924, p. 116.   [19] Ibid., dated 4/7/24, pp. 115–16.
[20] Ibid., dated Summer 1927, p. 123.
[21] Letters to Lydia Keynes, 1925–7, *Keynes Papers*, King's College Library, Cambridge, PP/45/190.
[22] Wittgenstein, *Letters to Russell, Keynes, and Moore*, dated March 29, 1924, p. 117. Wittgenstein replied "The answer is, No: there's nothing that can be done in that way, because I myself no longer have any strong inner drive to that sort of activity," ibid., dated 4/7/24, p. 116.
[23] *Collected Works*, vol. 10, p. 337.

branch of logic, held by both Moore and Keynes."[24] Whereas Keynes and Moore had conceived ethics as a field of inquiry in which one had to describe clearly the phenomenological essence of our concepts, Wittgenstein had held the view "that ethics cannot be put into words"; for Wittgenstein, "ethics is transcendental."[25] In short, for the early period I must concur with Skidelsky's assessment: "Whether [Wittgenstein] and Keynes developed any real intellectual rapport may be doubted."[26] There was some interest in each others' intellectual lives, but little substantive discussion.

After writing the *Tractatus* Wittgenstein retired from philosophy for ten years. He believed himself to have solved the problems of philosophy, leaving nothing left to do. In the preface he had written:

On the other hand the *truth* of the thoughts that are here communicated seems to me unassailable and definitive. I therefore believe myself to have found, on all essential points, the final solution of the problems.[27]

And to Keynes he confessed "Everything that I really *had* to say, I have said, and so the spring has run dry."[28] During this period, until 1929, the two did not correspond about, or discuss, philosophical questions. However, the few letters they did write, and Wittgenstein's visit to stay with Keynes in 1925, do indicate the strength of their friendship and the rapport they enjoyed when Wittgenstein did finally return to philosophy.

During his absence from Cambridge Wittgenstein expressed fears that a distance had grown between him and his English friends. Beginning in 1923 Keynes made repeated attempts to encourage Wittgenstein to visit England, even sending him money to pay for the trip, although he preferred to remain an anonymous donor of the money. Frank Ramsey, in a letter to Wittgenstein in December 1923, informed him:

First, the £50 belong to Keynes. He asked me not to say so straight away because he was afraid you might be less likely to take it from him than from an unknown source, as he has never written to you. I can't

---

[24] *Keynes. Hopes Betrayed*, p. 266. Keynes also referred to a certain difference in morality between the two in "My Early Beliefs," where he confessed: "We lacked reverence, as Lawrence observed and as Ludwig with justice also used to say – for everything and everyone," *Collected Works*, vol. 10, pp. 447–8.

[25] *Tractatus*, 6.421.

[26] *Keynes: Hopes Betrayed*, p. 266. [27] *Tractatus*, p. 4.

[28] Wittgenstein, *Letters to Russell, Keynes, and Moore*, dated 4/7/24, p. 116.

understand why he hasn't written, nor can he explain, he says he must have some 'complex' about it. He *speaks of you with warm affection and very much wants to see you again.* And also, apart from that, if you would like to come to England he would not like you to be unable to for want of money, of which he has plenty.[29]

Wittgenstein declined the invitation, explaining to Keynes

We haven't met since 11 years. I don't know if you have changed during that time, but *I* certainly have tremendously . . . And therefore if we shall meet you may find that the man who has come to see you isn't really the one you meant to invite.[30]

At this time Ramsey went to visit Wittgenstein in Austria, and tried to persuade him to make the trip. Ramsey, in a letter to Keynes, communicated Wittgenstein's reluctance, but also indicated the special position Keynes held with Wittgenstein at the time: "The people in England he wants to see are few; Russell he can no longer talk to, Moore he had some misunderstanding with, and there really only remain you and Hardy, and perhaps Johnson."[31] Later, in 1925, Wittgenstein warmed to the idea of a visit, and felt more optimistic about re-establishing contact with his friends. To Keynes he wrote "I'm not yet quite decided about whether I shall come or not but I should rather like to, if I could also see *you* during my stay."[32] And in a letter to W. Eccles earlier in 1925 he wrote:

Last summer I should have come to England to see a friend of mine Mr. Keynes (whose name you may know) in Cambridge. He would have paid my expenses, but I resolved after all not to come, because I was so much afraid that the long time and the great events (external and internal) that lie between us would prevent us from understanding one another. However now – or at least *to-day* I feel as if I might still be able to make myself understood by my old friends and if I get any opportunity I might – w.w.p. come and see you at Manchester.[33]

In August 1925 Wittgenstein did visit England, making arrangements before departure for Keynes to meet him: "Please let me

---

[29] In Ludwig Wittgenstein, *Letters to C. K. Ogden, with Comments on the English Translation of the Tractatus Logico-Philosophicus*, edited by G. H. von Wright (Oxford: Basil Blackwell, 1973), p. 82.

[30] Wittgenstein, *Letters to Russell, Keynes, and Moore*, dated 4/7/24, p. 115.

[31] Ibid., dated 24/3/24, p. 117.

[32] Ibid, dated 8/7/25, p. 119.

[33] W. Eccles, "Some Letters of Ludwig Wittgenstein," *Hermathena* 97 (1963), dated 10.3.25, pp. 60–1.

meet you in London as I don't like the idea of travelling about England alone now . . . I'm awfully curious how we are going to get on with one another."[34] And later in the trip he stayed with Keynes in Sussex: "I am in England, staying with Keynes, but as far from clarity as ever."[35]

After this visit Wittgenstein returned to Austria until early 1929 when doubts about his *Tractatus* led him back to Cambridge, and back to philosophy. As is evident from his correspondence during the twenties, Keynes was perhaps his closest friend at the time of his return. Keynes met him at the train, humorously recounting to Lydia: "Well, God has arrived. I met him on the 5.15 train."[36] He stayed as Keynes's guest at King's College for a couple of weeks, during which time Keynes gave a dinner to celebrate Wittgenstein's re-election to the Apostles.[37] Keynes was thus something of a social co-ordinator, a position Ramsey recognized when writing

Can I do anything to entertain Wittgenstein? I don't feel at all sure he wants to see me again, but I should love to do anything I can. There are lots of problems I should like his opinion on, though I fear he will find me so intolerably stupid that he won't want to talk about them.[38]

Keynes evidently enjoyed a privileged friendship with Wittgenstein at the beginning of the period leading up to the *Investigations*. The friendship also involved a great deal of discussion. Keynes tells of these in his letters to Lydia, writing that "I must not let him talk to me for more than two or three hours a day."[39] Later, he reported that they had "established a way of life which gives me a reasonable amount of free time."[40] These discussions continued throughout the next few years, as Keynes regularly referred to the "visits from Ludwig."[41] Keynes's letters also suggest that the discussions were often heated. In many of his letters to Lydia, when reporting on meetings with Wittgenstein, he would comment on whether or not the meeting featured a quarrel. Referring to a meeting in 1933 he wrote: "I enjoyed it but came away a little battered."[42] And later in

[34] Wittgenstein, *Letters to Russell, Keynes, and Moore*, dated July or August 1925, p. 120.
[35] Paul Engelmann, *Letters from Ludwig Wittgenstein. With a Memoir*, (Oxford: Basil Blackwell, 1967), p. 55. See also Wittgenstein, *Letters to Russell, Keynes and Moore*, footnote, p. 121.
[36] Letter of 1/18/29. Letters to Lydia, 1928–30.   [37] See Levy, *Moore*, p. 270.
[38] Letter of 10/1/29, *Keynes Papers*, King's College Library, JMK FR.
[39] Letter of 1/18/29. Letters to Lydia, 1928–30.   [40] Letter of 1/27/29, ibid.
[41] Letter of 12/4/33. Letters to Lydia, 1933–4.   [42] Letter of 2/12/33, ibid.

1934, he wrote of a "a terrific sense of leisure – which I am about to have destroyed by a visit from Ludwig after dinner to-night."[43] Other visits were less demanding, as when Keynes referred to a day which "included 1 1/2 hours of Ludwig who looked in to see me: however we didn't quarrel at all and it was a peaceful conversation."[44] On another occasion, he wrote; "Ludwig came to lunch today and we didn't quarrel at all."[45] Similarly, in the spring of 1932 he reported "Ludwig came and afterwards we went for a walk; – very peaceful and no strain for once."[46] However, the frequent debates implied by these letters are a testament to the strength of their friendship, rather than an indication of friction, and in 1935 Keynes was to describe Wittgenstein as "a very old and intimate friend of mine."[47] Wittgenstein was somewhat single-minded in his philosophizing, so it must be assumed that during these meetings throughout the early thirties Keynes and he were discussing philosophy. Skidelsky asks, "What did they talk about for two or three hours a day," and similarly concludes that "Much of the conversation must have been philosophical."[48] He also claims that Wittgenstein's return to Cambridge "had rekindled Keynes's love of philosophy."[49]

Besides the personal friendship between the two thinkers, Keynes was also involved in Wittgenstein's professional career. Throughout the thirties, Keynes maintained an interest in Wittgenstein's new work. Between 1929 and 1932 Wittgenstein delivered a series of influential lectures, and wrote a couple of manuscripts, incorporating a number of new ideas, included in which was his examination of the properties of vagueness. It was also during this time that the same discussion of vagueness creeps into Keynes's manuscripts. It is probable that Keynes picked up this analysis from Wittgenstein's work, and from the discussions in Cambridge surrounding it. At the end of 1931, when surveying Cambridge philosophy in an essay on Ramsey, Keynes indicated his awareness of Wittgenstein's latest work when he wrote "Wittgenstein is wondering if his next book will be finished before time's chariots are too near."[50] The book Keynes mentioned was

---

[43] Letter of 4/25/34, ibid.　　[44] Letter of 4/24/30. Letters to Lydia, 1928–30.
[45] Letter of 1/19/31. Letters to Lydia, 1931–2.　　[46] Letter of 4/24/32, ibid.
[47] Wittgenstein, *Letters to Russell, Keynes, and Moore*, p. 136.
[48] *Keynes. The Economist as Saviour*, p. 292.
[49] Ibid., p. 380.　　[50] *Collected Works*, vol. 10, p. 337.

probably a manuscript that Wittgenstein did not in the end publish, but which was published posthumously as the *Philosophical Remarks*.[51] It contained many of the transitional ideas Wittgenstein had developed in discussion with Ramsey, and delivered in his lectures.

Keynes's involvement continued throughout the decade. Later, in 1935, we find Wittgenstein apologizing to Keynes: "I'm sorry I must trouble you with my affairs again."[52] The affairs in question refer, according to Georg Henrik von Wright, "to the fact that Wittgenstein in the spring of 1935 had been discussing with Keynes his plans of publishing the book on which he was then working."[53] Keynes had offered financial assistance to enable Wittgenstein to publish a work dealing with his abandonment of many of the central ideas of the *Tractatus*, a work known at the time as *The Brown Book*.[54] In March of 1935 Keynes wrote to Moore:

I hear from Wittgenstein that he is anxious to publish the book he is writing under the auspices of the British Academy in the shape, I suppose, of a communication to them. I gather from him that you have given him a little encouragement, at any rate to the extent of not turning down the idea as impracticable. He seems very keen about this, so I should like to help it forward if I can.

If, therefore, the question of the Academy taking or not taking it were to depend at all on the question of expense, I would be ready to make a contribution to its cost by making a donation of, say, £50 to the Funds of the Academy.[55]

This project was soon abandoned as Wittgenstein moved on instead towards the *Philosophical Investigations*. The first sections of the book were circulated in manuscript form around the end of '38, beginning of '39. Wittgenstein at this time applied for the chair of philosophy after Moore's resignation. Keynes was one of the electors and asked Wittgenstein for the manuscript. In a letter to

---

[51] During the thirties Wittgenstein made several attempts to publish his new material, but abandoned the projects as he moved on instead towards the *Investigations*. For the chronology of these manuscripts see Georg Henrik von Wright, "The Wittgenstein Papers," *The Philosophical Review*, 78, (1969), pp. 483–503; as well as his "The Origin and Composition of Wittgenstein's Investigations," in *Wittgenstein: Sources and Perspectives*, edited by C. G. Luckhardt (Ithaca: Cornell University Press, 1979).

[52] Wittgenstein, *Letters to Russell, Keynes, and Moore*, dated 6/30/35, p. 132.

[53] Ibid., p. 133.

[54] Published later as part of the *Blue and Brown Books*.

[55] Letter of 3/6/35. *Keynes Papers*, King's College Library, Cambridge, PP/45/349.

Moore, Wittgenstein wrote "I had a p(ost) c(ard) on Wednesday from Keynes saying that he would like to see the English version of my book, or whatever is ready of it."[56] In the same letter Wittgenstein also recommended that Moore discuss the manuscript with Keynes as he was worried about the quality of the translation:

I have written to Keynes that you have read the first half of my first volume and could give him some information about it; for obviously you must be able to get more out of reading the original than Keynes could get out of a bad translation *and in a hurry*. So I *hope* he'll ask you to give him your opinion.[57]

Then to Keynes he wrote:

I went round to King's College last night with the M.S. but was told you had gone to London: so I took it back again and shall keep it till Friday unless you want it before then . . . I'm afraid there's *only one* copy of the English in existence and only one *corrected* copy of the German; you'll get these two copies.[58]

Wittgenstein was quite concerned about the whole affair, and wanted Keynes to get a good copy of the manuscript: "I went through it . . . , as far as I could in these two days, and corrected it almost word for word."[59] Keynes was thus one of the first to read the manuscript. After he had returned it, Wittgenstein wrote back, "Thanks for your kind notes. Yes, the translation is pretty awful."[60]

Unfortunately these notes do not exist, but Rush Rhees, translator of the manuscript, recounted in conversation that "Keynes wrote extremely enthusiastically about the first part of the *Investigations*."[61] And von Wright, a close friend of Wittgenstein, remembers: "I recollect one thing which Wittgenstein told me about Keynes's reaction to his manuscript. This was that Keynes had very much liked the comparison of the philosophers task to that of the psychotherapist."[62] Similarly, Bouwsma, recounting a conversation with Wittgenstein, reported the same reaction:

---

[56] Wittgenstein, *Letters to Russell, Keynes, and Moore*, dated 2/2/39, p. 176.
[57] Ibid., dated 2/2/39, p. 176.   [58] Ibid., dated 1/2/39, p. 138.
[59] Ibid., dated 3/2/39, p. 139.   [60] Ibid., dated 8/2/39, p. 140.
[61] Rush Rhees, telephone conversation, Swansea, July, 1986.
[62] G. H. von Wright, personal letter to the author from Helsinki, August, 14, 1986.

When [Wittgenstein] became a professor at Cambridge he submitted a typescript to the committee. Keynes was a member of the committee. Of 140 pages, 72 were devoted to the idea that philosophy is like psycho-analysis. A month later Keynes met him and said he was impressed with the idea that philosophy is psycho-analysis.[63]

Keynes liked the manuscript and supported Wittgenstein's application. After succeeding Moore as Professor of Philosophy Wittgenstein wrote to Keynes: "Thanks for the telegram, and thanks for all the trouble you've gone to. I hope to God that you haven't made a mistake. I know, it's up to me to prove that you haven't. Well, I *hope* I'll be a decent prof."[64]

While Wittgenstein and Keynes enjoyed a close friendship there is little to suggest that Keynes contributed at all to Wittgenstein's later ideas; and Wittgenstein, when later briefly commenting on Keynes's philosophy, only mentions his earlier work. In his lectures of Lent term, 1935, when considering the view of Russell and Frege that "logic is like a natural science"[65] he said:

Like a natural science, it could supposedly discover certain relations. For example, Keynes claimed to discover a probability relation which was like implication, yet not quite implication. But logic is a calculus, not a natural science, and in it one can make inventions but not discoveries.[66]

Indeed, there is even evidence that Wittgenstein thought Keynes misunderstood his philosophy. When Keynes asked for the manuscript of the *Investigations* Wittgenstein derisively commented to Moore, "I needn't say the whole thing is absurd as he couldn't make head or tail of it if it were translated very well."[67] Von Wright remembers that Keynes was impressed with the comparison in the manuscript of philosophy with psychoanalysis, but that Wittgenstein "seemed to have been rather annoyed at this reaction. He was anxious to play down the comparison."[68] This concern of

---

63 *Wittgenstein: Conversations*, p. 36.

64 Wittgenstein, *Letters to Russell, Keynes, and Moore*, dated 11/2/39, p. 141. Wittgenstein became professor on 11 February 1939.

65 *Wittgenstein's Lectures, Cambridge, 1932–35*, edited by Alice Ambrose (Oxford: Basil Blackwell, 1979), p. 139

66 Ibid. He returns to this point in the *Investigations*, sect. 109. Wittgenstein at this time would certainly also have objected to that part of Keynes's account of probability which involved postulating a direct, unanalyzable intuition of relations, for much the same reasons that he came to criticize Moore's use of intuition.

67 Wittgenstein, *Letters to Russell, Keynes, and Moore*, dated 2/2/39, p. 176.

68 Letter to the author, August 14, 1986, Helsinki.

Wittgenstein's dated back to the period of the *Blue and Brown Books*, when commentators first began to take the analogy too literally. Norman Malcolm recounts, "I believe another thing that angered him was the suggestion that in his conception philosophy was a form of psycho-analysis, a suggestion that I heard him explicitly attack, on two occasions, as based on a confusion. 'They are different techniques,' he had said."[69] However, not much weight should be placed on these scattered comments of Wittgenstein's as indicating his regard for Keynes's intellect. They should be seen in light of other similar ones made about most of the Cambridge philosophers. Of Moore, to whom the comment on Keynes was made, Wittgenstein once said to F. R. Leavis "he shows you how far a man can go who has absolutely no intelligence whatever."[70] About Ramsey he dismissively said "*He* can see the next step if you point it out";[71] and elsewhere called him a "bourgeois thinker," one who could only tinker with an intellectual edifice rather than reconstruct it.[72] And Russell's introduction to the *Tractatus* had caused Wittgenstein to long ago write him off. And yet all three had influenced Wittgenstein's thought in profound ways: Russell the *Tractatus*, Ramsey the *Investigations*, and Moore *On Certainty*. Indeed, Wittgenstein did not believe anyone understood what he was up to. The preface to the *Investigations* expresses the hope that the work will "bring light into one brain or another," but pessimistically adds "of course, it is not likely." So Wittgenstein's belittling comments on Keynes should be seen as standard treatment for his intellectual colleagues.[73] Lastly, Wittgenstein's assessment of whether someone understood his ideas is not particularly relevant to answering the question of whether or not that person was influenced by Wittgenstein. And Keynes, it should now be obvious, certainly was.

---

69 *Memoir*, pp. 56–7.
70 *The Critic As Anti-Philosopher*, edited by G. Singh (Athens: University of Georgia Press, 1982), p. 130. Leavis confesses that he is not sure the comment was made to him. It was perhaps an anecdote he had heard.
71 Ibid., p. 129.
72 See Monk, *Wittgenstein*, pp. 259–60.
73 Braithwaite also came in for rough treatment. He had written a survey of Cambridge philosophy for *University Studies, Cambridge 1933*, edited by Harold Wright (London: Ivor Nicholson & Watson, 1933), pp. 1–32, in which he discussed Wittgenstein's new ideas. Wittgenstein uncharacteristically published a letter in which he disclaimed "all responsibility for the views and thoughts which Mr. Braithwaite attributes to me." *Mind* 42 (1933), p. 415.

It is evident that Keynes maintained an involvement in the intellectual life of Wittgenstein, was aware of the work he was doing, and considered it of importance to facilitate his continued publication. This makes it highly likely that Keynes's later analysis of vagueness and ordinary language derived to some extent from the work Wittgenstein was doing during the first half of the thirties. Furthermore, the story of Keynes's involvement with Cambridge philosophy becomes more complete when we add his friendship with two other colleagues who had a significant influence on Wittgenstein – Ramsey and Sraffa.

RAMSEY

The importance of Ramsey's criticisms to Wittgenstein's ideas provides another clue in piecing together Keynes's involvement in the Cambridge philosophical community, for it is obvious from Keynes's eulogy essay that he was well acquainted with Ramsey's philosophy.[74] This is significant because in the preface to the *Investigations* Wittgenstein pays tribute to the forceful criticisms of Frank Ramsey:

For since beginning to occupy myself with philosophy again, sixteen years ago, I have been forced to recognize grave mistakes in what I wrote in that first book. I was helped to realize these mistakes – to a degree which I myself am hardly able to estimate – by the criticism which my ideas encountered from Frank Ramsey, with whom I discussed them in innumerable conversations during the last two years of his life.[75]

K. T. Fann claims that Ramsey's logical pragmatism contributed to the "decidedly pragmatic tendency in Wittgenstein's later work."[76] Ramsey, while paying tribute in return to the influence of

---

[74] "Ramsey as a Philosopher," in *Collected Works*, vol 10, pp. 336–9.
[75] *Investigations*, p. viii. The two years in question were 1928–30.
[76] *Wittgenstein's Conception of Philosophy*, p. 47. Wittgenstein has been labeled a pragmatist. See Rorty, *Consequences of Pragmatism*, introduction. Rorty argues that pragmatism was "waiting at the end of the dialectical road which analytic philosophy traveled" (p. xviii). Keynes too has been placed in that tradition. See Dudley Dillard, "The Pragmatic Basis of Keynes's Political Economy," *Journal of Economic History*, (November 1946), pp. 121–52; Allan G. Gruchy, "The Philosophical Basis of the New Keynesian Economics," *Ethics*, 58 (July 1948), pp. 235–44; P. V. Mini, *Philosophy and Economics*. (Gainesville: University Presses of Florida, 1974), chs. 12–15; and Baldwin Ranson, "Rival Economic Epistemologies: The Logics of Marx, Marshall, and Keynes," *Journal of Economic Issues*, 14 (1980), pp. 77–98.

Wittgenstein, indicated his departure from Wittgenstein's earlier logic:

I must emphasize my indebtedness to Mr. Wittgenstein, from whom my view of logic is derived. Everything that I have said is due to him, except the parts which have a pragmatist tendency, which seem to me to be needed in order to fill up a gap in his system.[77]

Ramsey's pragmatism comes out clearly in his criticisms of Keynes's *Treatise of Probability*. Ramsey denied the possibility of intuiting probability relations. In a passage that may have led to Keynes's later comments in "My Early Beliefs" about how the Apostles argued about differing interpretations of objects given directly in consciousness, Ramsey claimed:

[Keynes] supposes that . . . [probability relations] can be perceived; but speaking for myself I feel confident that this is not true. I do not perceive them, and if I am to be persuaded that they exist it must be by argument; moreover I shrewdly suspect that others do not perceive them either, because they are able to come to so very little agreement as to which of them relates any two given propositions.[78]

Ramsey's pragmatism on these matters is conspicuous in his treatment of induction for he maintained that it "could not be reduced to deductive inference or justified by formal logic."[79] Moreover, he did not find this state of affairs "a scandal to philosophy" for induction receives all the justification it needs from the fact that it is a "useful habit" which "lead[s] on the whole to true opinions";[80] accepting the conclusions of induction is thus "reasonable," even if not "rational," i.e. justifiable by formal logic.[81] Ramsey claimed "This is a kind of pragmatism: we judge mental habits by whether they work, i.e. whether the opinions they lead to

---

[77] "Facts and Propositions," in *The Foundations of Mathematics*, p. 155.
[78] "Truth and Probability," in *Foundations*, p. 161.
[79] Ibid., pp. 196–7.
[80] Ibid.
[81] In drawing a distinction between the rational and the reasonable, Ramsey was making much the same point as the philosophers of the New Rhetoric are making today. Chaim Perelman, for example, says "the existence of two adjectives, 'rational' and 'reasonable,' both derived from the same noun, and designating a conformity with reason, would pose no problem if the two terms were interchangeable. But, most often, it is not so." The rational, he says, "corresponds to mathematical reason," while the reasonable man "is influenced by *common sense*." "The Rational and the Reasonable," in *The New Rhetoric and the Humanities* (Dordrecht: D. Reidel, 1979), pp. 117–18.

are for the most part true, or more often true than those which alternative habits would lead to."[82]

Ramsey, like the later Wittgenstein, questioned the utility of formal logic as an instrument for analyzing our thought patterns. He pointed out that while "it is contended that formal logic or the logic of consistency is the whole of logic,"[83] he suggested "let us . . . try to get an idea of a human logic which shall not attempt to be reducible to formal logic."[84] When looking into "human logic," Ramsey considered the case of "mathematical propositions whose truth or falsity cannot as yet be decided" even though "it may humanly speaking be right to entertain a certain degree of belief in them."[85] In this case "a logic which proposes to justify such a degree of belief must be prepared actually to go against formal logic; for to a formal truth formal logic can only assign a degree of belief 1."[86] He continued: "This point seems to me to show particularly clearly that human logic or the logic of truth, which tells men how they should think, is not merely independent of but sometimes actually incompatible with formal logic."[87]

Ramsey claimed that "we have . . . to consider the human mind and what is the most we can ask of it."[88] His arguments for this approach may have caused Wittgenstein to examine the actual use of language, his language games. Ramsey may thus have led Wittgenstein to recognize the divergence between his earlier logical apparatus and our natural language, and to see that language can indeed function without the logical properties the analytics thought were necessary. Keynes quoted a passage from Ramsey which is critical of the arcane logical ideals of the *Tractatus*, and which even suggests the possibility that the later concern in Cambridge philosophy with the analysis of vagueness may have begun with Ramsey:

---

[82] "Truth and Probability," pp. 197–8.
[83] Ibid., p. 190.   [84] Ibid., p. 193.
[85] Ibid., p. 191.   [86] Ibid.
[87] Ibid., p. 191. Perelman also notes that "in certain cases the rational and the reasonable are in precise opposition" ("The Rational," p. 117). He takes as an example of this Wittgenstein's argument, in *On Certainty*, that Descartes's rational doubt is in fact unreasonable.
[88] "Truth and Probability," p. 194.

The chief danger to our philosophy, apart from laziness and woolliness, is *scholasticism*, the essence of which is treating what is vague as if it were precise and trying to fit it into an exact logical category.[89]

This passage was aimed specifically at Tractarian notions such as: "Without philosophy thoughts are, as it were, cloudy and indistinct: its task is to make them clear and to give them sharp boundaries."[90] Ramsey had earlier discussed the issue of vagueness with Russell, and reported to Wittgenstein that Russell "*indignantly denied ever having said that vagueness* is a characteristic of *the physical world.*" [91] Later he focused on the property as one which challenged much of analytic philosophy. He spoke, for example, about "the vagueness of the whole idea of understanding";[92] and elsewhere he claimed "there is no point in fixing on a precise sense of 'reasonable,'" subsequently indicating all the different ways the word can be used.[93]

Keynes may thus have picked up his analysis of vagueness from either Wittgenstein or Ramsey at this stage. In his lecture of November 6, 1933 Keynes is recorded as paraphrasing Ramsey very closely when he said "In a complicated subject like economics the thing to do is avoid woolliness on the one hand, and scholasticism on the other."[94] Furthermore, Laurie Tarshis, one of the students recording the lectures, wrote of scholasticism, "'the essence of which is treating what is vague as what is precise.'"[95] The fact that he put this passage in quotation marks indicates perhaps that Keynes made it clear that he was quoting, obviously from Ramsey. The influence of Ramsey is also supported by Keynes's many comments indicating respect for his intellect. Even when Ramsey was an undergraduate Keynes took his views seriously. At that time Keynes described him to Broad as "an infant, aged about 18, and cannot remember life before the war,"[96] but "certainly far and away the most brilliant undergraduate who has appeared for many years in the border-country between Philosophy and Mathematics."[97] Harrod, when discussing Keynes's and Ramsey's friendship,

---

[89] Quoted in *Collected Works*, vol. 10, p. 343.   [90] *Tractatus*, 4.112.

[91] In Wittgenstein, *Letters to C. K. Ogden*, dated 2/20/24, p. 84.

[92] "Philosophy," in *Foundations*, p. 264.

[93] "Further Considerations," in *Foundations*, p. 199.

[94] *Keynes's Lectures*, p. 102.   [95] Ibid., p. 101.

[96] Letter of 2/4/22, *Keynes Papers*, King's College, Cambridge, TP/1/1 Box 18.

[97] Letter of 1/31/22, ibid.

recounted that "Keynes assured me that [Ramsey] was as good a philosopher as anyone living."[98] Harrod further recorded that "Ramsey's criticisms of his theory of Probability . . . [Keynes] took more seriously than any others."[99] And after Ramsey's death in 1930 Keynes wrote to Lydia: "Frank Ramsey died last night . . . He was in his way the greatest genius in the College."[100] As a tribute, Keynes published two eulogies, one dealing with Ramsey's contributions to economics and the other with his philosophical work. Keynes's interest continued after these pieces, and towards the end of 1932 he suggested to Braithwaite the project of making an anthology of Ramsey's writings.[101] Braithwaite approved of the idea, and in the course of discussing the materials to be included they both expressed interest in the idea that philosophy is a form of therapy, that, as Ramsey wrote, "instead of answering questions, it aims merely at curing headaches."[102] Wittgenstein had much the same view of philosophy, one that Keynes had agreed with, but it appears Keynes came across the idea first in Ramsey's work. Much of Keynes's understanding of later Cambridge philosophy could thus be due to Ramsey.

SRAFFA

The story so far can be rounded out by considering the other Cambridge economist closely connected with philosophy at that time, Piero Sraffa. In the preface to the *Investigations*, Wittgenstein thanks Sraffa even more than Ramsey for the criticisms which helped effect the transition to his later doctrines: "I am indebted to this stimulus for the most consequential ideas of this book."[103]

---

[98] *Keynes*, p. 321.   [99] Ibid.
[100] Letter of 1/19/30. Letters to Lydia, 1928–30.
[101] See Letter from Braithwaite to Keynes, 12/25/32, *Keynes Papers*, King's College Library, JMK FR. The two eulogies and the short anthology are published together in Keynes's *Collected Works*, vol. 10, pp. 335–46.
[102] *Collected Works*, vol. 10, p. 343. See also the letter from Braithwaite of 1/14/33, *Keynes Papers*, King's College Library, JMK FR.
[103] *Investigations*, p. viii. As a further indication of how closely knit the group of Cambridge thinkers was, Sraffa, in the preface to his own book, wrote "I am also indebted for . . . help at different periods to the late Mr Frank Ramsey," *Production of Commodities by Means of Commodities: Prelude to a Critique of Economic Theory* (Cambridge University Press, 1960), p. vii. Jean Piere Potier provides a rounded story of Sraffa's involvement with the Cambridge economists and philosophers in *Piero Sraffa – Unorthodox Economist (1898–1983). A Biographical Essay* (London: Routledge, 1991).

There is a story connected with this collaboration, one which has become something of a legend. This took place while Wittgenstein and Sraffa were arguing out the ideas of the *Tractatus*. Without going into the details of the philosophical point at issue in the discussion, they were disputing the Tractarian notion that language serves one basic function, that of stating factual propositions, and that this function is made possible because the structure of propositions shares the same "logical form" as the structure of facts. Norman Malcolm recounts the story:

One day (they were riding, I think, on a train) when Wittgenstein was insisting that a proposition and that which it describes must have the same "logical form," the same "logical multiplicity," Sraffa made a gesture, familiar to Neapolitans as meaning something like disgust or contempt, of brushing the underneath of his chin with an outward sweep of the finger-tips of one hand. And he asked: 'What is the logical form of that?' Sraffa's example produced in Wittgenstein the feeling that there was an absurdity in the insistence that a proposition and what it describes must have the same "form." This broke the hold on him of the conception that a proposition must literally be a 'picture' of the reality it describes.[104]

Put another way, it made Wittgenstein realize that language serves more functions that just stating facts; we also do things with language, like express disgust. Fann, commenting on this anecdote, points out that "this particular criticism in itself does not constitute a decisive 'counter-example' (for according to the *Tractatus*, the gesture does not constitute a 'proposition')."[105] However, Fann continues, "it was probably a series of this *kind* of concrete counter-example which broke the hold on Wittgenstein of the conception that language always functions in *one* way."[106]

Keynes too was a close friend of Sraffa. Keynes had invited Sraffa to teach in the economics faculty, an offer that was accepted towards the end of 1927. Upon Sraffa's arrival in Cambridge Keynes organized living arrangements and dining rights at King's College. The two later organized the Circus, a discussion group that met in 1930 and '31 to argue out the ideas that led to the *General Theory*. Sraffa was also one of the main critics of the early manuscripts of that book. Furthermore, Keynes's and Sraffa's friendship was not confined to economic matters, as they shared a passion for book

---

[104] Malcolm, *Memoir*, p. 69.
[105] *Wittgenstein's Conception of Philosophy*, p. 48.　　[106] Ibid., pp. 48–9.

collecting. In 1938 they co-authored the introduction to an *Abstract of Hume's Treatise of Human Nature* in which they identified the author as Hume himself, and not Adam Smith as had been previously believed. Given their close collaboration, one that extended to writing a piece on the history of philosophy, it is likely that discussion would frequently drift to the latest ideas of Wittgenstein. Moreover, Sraffa's philosophical ideas, which influenced Wittgenstein so profoundly, would certainly also have had some sort of impress on Keynes. Fann has argued that Sraffa's method may have had an effect on Wittgenstein, and this method Keynes had encountered back in 1928 when, as Sraffa recounted, "Lord Keynes read a draft of the opening propositions" of his book.[107]

It is difficult to say anything about Sraffa's philosophical views, as he never wrote anything on the subject. He lamented, "I have never written anything on philosophy or Wittgenstein. If I ever tried this I doubt that I should ever complete it."[108] But Sraffa and Keynes were particularly well-suited to spot fallacies in the formidable structure of analytic philosophy: on the one hand, they were both familiar with the work being done in Cambridge, but on the other, not being primarily philosophers, they enjoyed a certain distance from the logical model then capturing the imaginations of analytic philosophers. Keynes in the *Treatise on Probability* recognized the appeal of Russell's method when he wrote: "As a method of setting forth the system of formal truth, which shall possess beauty, inter-dependence, and completeness, his is vastly superior to any which has preceded it."[109] But he immediately followed this observation with his reservations by questioning "the relation in which ordinary reasoning stands to this ordered system."[110] Wittgenstein later concluded "the conflict becomes intolerable; the requirement is now in danger of becoming empty."[111] Perhaps that is why Keynes and Sraffa were well placed to help the movement along – they were not caught-up by the logical ideal, or with each new sophistication which promised to solve the conundrums of analysis. And perhaps it was their common sense, coupled with an understanding of

---

[107] *Production of Commodities by Means of Commodities*, p. vi. See Fann, *Wittgenstein's Conception of Philosophy*, p. 49.
[108] Quoted in Fann, *Wittgenstein's Conception of Philosophy*, p. 48, fn. 2.
[109] *Collected Works*, vol. 8, p. 128.
[110] Ibid.   [111] *Investigations*, sect. 107.

philosophy, that caused the Cambridge philosophers to be slightly in awe of, even intimidated by, the economists. Von Wright has recounted that:

> It was above all Sraffa's acute and forceful criticism that compelled Wittgenstein to abandon his earlier views and set out upon new roads. He said that his discussions with Sraffa made him feel like a tree from which all branches had been cut.[112]

Russell as well came away from discussions with Keynes feeling that his philosophy was a touch far-fetched:

> Keynes intellect was the sharpest and clearest that I have ever known. When I argued with him, I felt that I took my life in my hands, and I seldom emerged without feeling something of a fool.[113]

Keynes's common sense attitude to analytic philosophy led him to consider the divergence between logic and language as central for Cambridge philosophy during its transitional phase. In his essay on Ramsey he focused on the same "systematic divergence" as Wittgenstein did:

> The first impression conveyed by the work of Russell was that the field of formal logic was enormously extended. The gradual perfection of the formal treatment [of logic] at the hands of [Russell], of Wittgenstein and of Ramsey had been, however, gradually to empty it of content and to reduce it more and more to mere dry bones, until finally it seemed to exclude not only all experience, but most of the principles, usually reckoned logical, of reasonable thought.[114]

Keynes, however, goes on from this assessment of Ramsey's early work to indicate, and to praise, "how far his mind was departing . . . from the formal and objective treatment of his immediate predecessors."[115] Specifically, Keynes recounted that Ramsey "was led to consider 'human logic' as distinguished from 'formal logic,'"[116] and in so doing "may have been pointing the way to the next field of study when formal logic has been put into good order and its highly limited scope properly defined."[117] He said Ramsey had come to display a "common sense and a sort of hard-headed

[112] "Biographical Sketch," in Malcolm, *Memoir*, p. 15.
[113] Bertrand Russell, *Autobiography. Vol. 1: 1872–1914* (London: George Allen & Unwin, 1967), p. 72.
[114] *Collected Works*, vol. 10, p. 338.   [115] Ibid.
[116] Ibid.   [117] Ibid., p. 339.

practicality towards the whole business."[118] Keynes evidently had in mind the course Cambridge philosophy was then taking, be it in the form of Wittgenstein's defense of our natural language, or Ramsey's vindication of "reasonable" mental habits against the restrictions of formal logic.

In conclusion to this discussion of the relationship between Keynes and the Cambridge philosophers I would say that there is a sufficient amount of evidence, both biographical and textual, to support the thesis that Keynes was influenced by the ideas of later Cambridge philosophy. His comments on language indicate that Wittgenstein exerted the strongest influence, but he could also have learned of the new ideas from Ramsey and Sraffa. Keynes, Ramsey and Wittgenstein all followed roughly parallel routes in escaping from the formative ideals of analytic philosophy. Keynes may have begun his philosophical career under the sway of Russell and Moore, but this influence, and the credibility of their rationalism, waned for him and for Cambridge generally. This is not to say that Moore played no role in later Cambridge philosophy. He attended Wittgenstein's lectures during the early thirties, and published an important account of them.[119] And Wittgenstein during this period valued Moore's understanding and expository skill. When Moore stopped attending the lectures in 1934, Wittgenstein wrote: "I wish to God you would attend my classes! It would give me ever so much more of a chance to make things clear, to you *and* to others. Would you come if I promised to provide a very comfortable chair and tobacco and pipecleaners?"[120] Furthermore, Moore's extensive discussions with Wittgenstein led to the manuscript, *On Certainty*. Indeed, much of what is characteristic of later Cambridge thought is an elaboration of at least the spirit of Moore's defense of common sense. However, it was in the course of discussing the newer ideas developed by his friends at Cambridge that Keynes's mature thoughts on language took shape. Skidelsky draws the same conclusion: "There is talk of a famous lunch at which Ramsey, Wittgenstein and Sraffa discussed probability with Keynes. It is hard not to believe that Keynes's intercourse with the

---

[118] Ibid.
[119] "Wittgenstein's Lectures in 1930–33," in *Philosophical Papers* (London: George Allen & Unwin, 1959), pp. 252–324.
[120] Wittgenstein, *Letters to Russell, Keynes, and Moore*, dated Monday, September 1934, p. 163.

most powerful philosophical minds of the day shook him out of his comfortable pre-war certainties."[121]

Keynes and Wittgenstein both reached the watershed between their early and late periods at roughly the same time, 1932–5. This was when Wittgenstein circulated his transitional *Blue and Brown Books*; and it was when Keynes hit upon the notion of effective demand. There is obviously no connection here. But it should be remembered that Keynes characterized his transition as "a struggle of escape from habitual modes of thought and expression," which implies a change in style as well as substance in his economics. This is documented in his lectures, correspondence, and articles during this period, as well as in the drafts of the *General Theory*. It is found as well in his essay on Malthus.[122] The essay was originally written in 1914 and revised in 1922, but several new sections were inserted in 1933 and indicate at least one of the subjects on Keynes's mind at the time. The new sections largely deal with questions of method, and specifically with the problem of relating symbolic models to reality. Here he begins his often repeated critique of Ricardo's mechanical methods and states his preference for the "vaguer intuitions of Malthus."[123] It is perhaps merely a coincidence that both thinkers began attacking reductive and formalized analyses at the same time, Wittgenstein the reductivism of analytic philosophy, Keynes that of symbolic social science. I do not think that Keynes's change in method was simply the result of his incorporating into his economics recent advances in Cambridge philosophy. What is more likely the case is that Keynes came to work out the implications that these philosophical insights held for economics when he later hit upon the notion of the consumption function, and subsequently that of effective demand and the theory of employment – the creation of macro-economics.

During Keynes's transitional phase the concern for methodological controversy emerged because the only way he could explain the "complete disappearance of the theory of the demand and supply for output as a whole, i.e. the theory of employment"[124] was

---

[121] *Keynes. The Economist As Saviour*, p. 292.   [122] *Collected Works*, vol. 10, pp. 71–108.
[123] Ibid., p. 88.   [124] *Collected Works*, vol. 14, p. 85.

because Ricardo's method was a "more fascinating intellectual construction"[125] than Malthus's, which appeared by comparison "very superficial."[126] The attempt to persuade the world of his economic theory was bound up with attacking inappropriate epistemic ideals; notions on method had a formative influence on substantive economics. It was the "intellectual domination"[127] of Ricardo's method that had "constrained the subject for a full hundred years in an artificial groove."[128] This was something which, Keynes wrote, "regarded historically [is] the most extraordinary thing,"[129] and on several occasions he puzzled over its occurrence. He speculated on its "complex of suitabilities,"[130] but the one feature to which he attached most importance was that "it was adapted to carry a vast and consistent logical superstructure," something which "gave it beauty."[131] Ricardo's "more rigid approach" of going "behind 'effective demand'" to specify the "fundamental factors" at work, and then showing them "as automatically working themselves out in a unique and unequivocal way"[132] proved a hegemonic methodological ideal. Keynes therefore came to examine the "cleavage between the conclusions of economic theory and those of common sense,"[133] much as he had commented on the systematic divergence between logical theory and everyday forms of reasoning. In both cases the pursuit of precision had driven the disciplines to unreasonable conclusions. It was at this time, and in reference to the rediscovery of the theory of employment, that Keynes declared that he was "returning to an age-long tradition of common sense."[134]

The conclusion that Keynes mechanically incorporated into his economics Wittgenstein's later philosophical insights must be denied. The coincidence of the timing of these two thinkers' transitions to their later thought was indeed just that – a coincidence. However, what is not a coincidence is the similarity between the critiques of formalization Keynes employed once he realized the need to attack epistemic ideals within economics, and those developed by Wittgenstein and Ramsey. The biographical evidence presented in this chapter, consisting as it does of evidence

125 *Collected Works*, vol. 10, p. 87.   126 Ibid., p. 88.
127 Ibid.   128 Ibid., p. 87.
129 *Collected Works*, vol. 14, p. 85.   130 *Collected Works*, vol. 7, p. 32.
131 Ibid., p. 33.   132 *Collected Works*, vol. 10, p. 88.
133 *Collected Works*, vol. 7, p. 350. See also p. 192.   134 *Collected Works*, vol. 13, p. 552.

that Keynes was closely involved with the ideas of Ramsey which influenced Wittgenstein, that he was not only meeting regularly with Wittgenstein throughout this period, but also reading his manuscripts, makes it highly unlikely that Keynes did not have first-hand knowledge of Wittgenstein's new ideas. This evidence, coupled with the textual evidence given in the previous chapters, shows that Keynes was indeed drawing upon the new ideas in Cambridge philosophy for his later position on language and method.

Conclusion: complexity, vagueness, and rhetoric

LOOKING FOR AN EXIT FROM LANGUAGE

As the formalizing and programmatic zeal of early analytic philosophy faded, Cambridge philosophy began drifting from its commitment to the ideal language of logical atomism. Ramsey and Wittgenstein were the leading apostates and began to focus on the recalcitrant vagueness of our common sense. Early in the thirties Keynes understood the import of the new ideas and extended them into the philosophy of the social sciences. Wittgenstein and Ramsey remain today influential philosophers, and their ideas continue to play a role in current debates. Keynes's contribution, however, charts out a position which should be given closer consideration in contemporary discussions of the philosophy of the social sciences. For it is of continued relevance in defending common sense against the criticisms voiced against it today by many positivists and philosophers of formal semantics, on the one hand, and by post-structuralists on the other. What these critics take to be a defect in natural language, its vagueness, Keynes took to be a valued property in simplifying theory. He has shown that the use of ordinary language does not leave us mired in contradiction and undisciplined thought. Between the alternatives of metaphorical *jouissance* and an austere canonical notation there is a middle route, and its viability has been argued for, and displayed, by Keynes.

Arguing for a role for ordinary language and common sense in the social sciences, however, involves defending forms of knowledge that philosophy has traditionally believed to be unreliable. These forms of knowledge run afoul of Russell's and Quine's view of the need for clear identity conditions for entities entering into theory. They would also seem to hinder the simplification of theory. Furthermore, the absence of indubitable starting-points, the absence of a universal method and claims to objectivity raise the spectre of rampant subjectivity which philosophy originally set out to tame. And the very mention of common sense suggests to some a reactionary stance of fossilizing current beliefs. Many of these views originated with Plato. He bequeathed to Western philosophy the assumption of a dichotomy between knowledge and belief: where reason cannot offer certain knowledge we have only stories, mythology. He thought we rose above the chaos of opinions in the market-place not through arguments within common sense and within our natural language, but by finding an exit from everyday language into a world of pure forms; this realm of unambiguous entities was the ancestor to Russell's and Quine's ideal languages. Philosophy since his time has been characterized by various efforts to find more secure starting-points for thought than Platonic forms. The assumption has persisted that true knowledge requires something more objective and ahistorical than the standards of truth agreed upon by a community of specialists in the course of discussion and argumentation. There has been in philosophy a shared lack of confidence in our ability to discipline our own thoughts, and consequently a search for some external check against the feared rampant subjectivity. Within the social sciences this manifests itself in their often inappropriate emulation of an idealized method of the natural sciences. However, in glorifying a single method as the only form of rational inquiry, philosophy has worked, many now feel, to limit all meaningful discourse to one form; it has, in Bernard Williams's words, set up "demands for a single currency of reasons."[1] Michael Oakeshott pointed out that

the view dies hard that Babel was the occasion of a curse being laid upon mankind from which it is the business of the philosophers to deliver us, and a disposition remains to impose a single character upon all significant human speech.[2]

---

[1] *Ethics and the Limits of Philosophy* (London: Fontana, 1985), p. 206, n. 13.

[2] *Rationalism in Politics and Other Essays* (New York: Basic Books, 1962), p. 197. Williams points out that "the demand for explicit discursive rationality is as old as Socrates, and does not represent any modern influence, but the most powerful models of justification now active ... are certainly expressions of modern bureaucratic rationality" (*Ethics and the Limits of Philosophy*, p. 206, n. 13). He thinks this "rationalistic conception of rationality" arose from "social features of the modern world" which "requires in principle every decision to be based on grounds that can be discursively explained" (ibid., p. 18). For discussions of the influence the modern state structure has had on forms of thought, see as well Georg Lukács, *History and Class Consciousness*; translated by Rodney Livingstone

A paradoxical result of this endeavor has been that the criteria of knowledge and truth often articulated by philosophy have been so stringent that no branch of learning, science included, has been able to live up to the standard. Thus, philosophy, which was originally conceived as a means to bring order into our knowledge, has often been driven to conclude that most of the questions we ask cannot be answered rationally. Hume's views as to the impossibility of rationally justifying ethical and aesthetic judgments, or of justifying the procedure of the empirical sciences is a good example of the paradox. Such was the substance of Isocrates' warning when philosophy first began: foremost teacher of rhetoric at the time of Plato, he warned that, while philosophy was a good disciplining study, its goals were unattainable, and worse, inimical to right living in society. Philosophy's sole concern with certainty, he said, has turned it into "a gymnastic of the mind," and "a training which is no help to us in the present either in our speech or in our actions."[3] Philosophy's project of improving our knowledge had become empty; its ideal was too lofty, unattainable. What had begun as a healthy desire to liberate positive knowledge from the binds of myth and religion had turned into a strait-jacket.

(London: Merlin Press, 1979); R. H.Tawney "Religious Thought on Social and Economic Questions in the Sixteenth and Seventeenth Centuries," Parts 1, 2, 3, *Journal of Political Economy* 31 (1923); Alexis de Tocqueville, "The Influences of Democracy Upon Philosophy," in *Democracy in America*, trans. Henry Reeve (London: Oxford University Press, 1946), pp. 295–303. Rorty, on the other hand, thinks reductionism is inherent in all philosophy since the Greeks. This has stemmed from the prevalent belief that knowledge is essentially a mirroring of the world: reductionism follows from any philosophy "dominated by Greek ocular metaphors," *Philosophy and the Mirror of Nature* (Princeton University Press, 1979), p. 11. Derrida makes much the same point, although from a different angle. He thinks Western philosophy has been primarily concerned with the certainty of intuitions ever since Plato tried to conceal the essential textuality of ideas and the written character of philosophy. Toulmin, on the other hand, suggests the opposite conclusion to Derrida's, that the invention of the printing-press caused philosophy to lose sight of the context-dependence of speech: "in a largely pre-literate world the transient firework-like character of our utterances would remain overwhelmingly obvious. The conception of the proposition as outlasting the moment of its utterance . . . would become plausible only after the permanent recorded word had come to play a much larger part in the lives of speculative men," *The Uses of Argument*, p. 181.

3 Isocrates, "Antidoxis," in *Loeb Classical Library*, vol. 2, *Isocrates*, translated by G. Norlin, edited by T. E. Page, E. Capps, and W. H. D. Rouse (London: William Heinemann, 1928), p. 333. It is surprising that Rorty does not invoke the name of Isocrates given the similarity of their critiques of philosophy. For Isocrates' critique see Samuel Ijsseling, *Rhetoric and Philosophy in Conflict: An Historical Survey* (The Hague: Martinus Nijhoff, 1976), chs. 3 and 4.

Consequently, philosophy since Plato has alternated between a strict rationalism and a romantic or irrational reaction which concluded that since reason is incapable of answering most the questions we ask then the world must be comprehended intuitively or artistically. Keynes commented on this false polarity in the *Treatise on Probability*, where, in discussing the usual requirement in metaphysics of deductive certainty, he pointed out that:

> transcendental philosophy has partly arisen, I believe, through the belief that there is no knowledge on these matters short of certain knowledge, being combined with the belief that such certain knowledge of metaphysical questions is beyond the power of ordinary methods.[4]

Between the extremes of an other-worldly rationalism and a romantic intuitionism of the Bergson variety there exists the common sense of individual sciences. Rorty makes this case in his ambitious critique of the imperialism of philosophy. The methodological reductionism of traditional philosophy must be abandoned for it no longer has a role to play. He thinks Wittgenstein, Derrida, Davidson, and Quine have shown that the specification of intuitions which hook onto bare reality is impossible. There is therefore no Truth, no defining property which all true statements such as "Murder is wrong," "2+2=4," and "The earth is round" share; there are just truths, arrived at by mundane, local considerations. Philosophy, Rorty argues, should just end, leaving the particular fields of substantive inquiry, in all their philosophical innocence.

Rorty has synthesized the ideas of a wide range of post-positivist philosophers into a contemporary defense of common sense. Arguing against the common assumption that all branches of thought should be modelled after physics, he claims it is misleading to say that science works because it describes the way the world is objectively, independent of our interpretive framework. Modern science points no epistemological or logical lesson, it is just a successful form of text, one among many. Bernard Williams, while sympathetic to a critique of philosophy's imperialism, thinks Rorty misunderstands the common sense of science itself. Williams argues that the notion of scientific inquiry being constrained by independent facts, rather than being the scene of textual licence, is one that does not originate from philosophy; it is one that derives

---

[4] *Collected Works*, vol. 8, p. 266.

"from within scientific reflection itself."[5] So it is incorrect to say that objectivist notions are the brainchild of modern philosophy. More importantly, it is not obvious that science has been misled by these supposedly philosophical ideas, as Rorty implies most modern thinkers have been. If pragmatism entails that ideas are defended by their convenience and utility, and if science's standards of inquiry have been constrained by a belief in an objective truth, then these ideas have proven their utility and should not be discarded, particularly, argues Williams, in favor of the textual image pushed by Rorty. Williams thus thinks Rorty has drawn the wrong conclusion from the philosophers he admires, such as Wittgenstein:

> If it is impossible to provide grounds for, or get beyond, what, at a very general level, we naturally say; and if philosophy, as traditionally understood, tried to go beyond that, and so should now end; why should it not *simply* end, so that all we should say is what anyway we naturally say?[6]

It is, however, questionable if we can be as philosophically naive in our thinking as this reading of Wittgenstein implies. Williams is surely right that science has not been misled by epistemology; but Rorty has accurately pointed out that many other disciplines have been under pressure, from largely philosophical sources, to remake the language they previously used. Williams recognizes this when he suggests that an area where Rorty's criticism has a valuable contribution to make is moral philosophy.[7] Perhaps the real work for Rorty's ideas, and for the analysis of common sense, lies outside of the philosophy of science. For in ethics, literary criticism, history, and the social sciences philosophy does have an influence on substantive practice in a way it does not in physics. Here philosophical reflection really has a point, it has an influence. For here the failure of experimental and formal techniques to achieve a consensus on method has left these disciplines in a permanent state of philosophical turmoil; and, while in the natural sciences methodology appeared on the scene after the fact of scientific discovery, in the social sciences the order of reflection is often the reverse.

This can be seen clearly in some of the original works of social

---

[5] "Auto-da-Fe: Consequences of Pragmatism," in *Reading Rorty*, p. 31.
[6] "Auto-da-Fe," p. 32. See "Wittgenstein and Idealism," in *Moral Luck* (Cambridge University Press, 1981), pp. 144–63, for Williams' reading of Wittgenstein.
[7] "Auto-da-Fe," pp. 35–6.

science which claimed to be scientific. The empirical and axiomatic methods were first adopted as a solution to the age-old problem of how to couch beliefs in a form or method that would give them an appearance of being something more than mere opinion. William Letwin has argued that these methods first emerged in economics at the time of the Recoinage Crisis. With the transfer of political power from king to parliament at that time it became increasingly difficult to convince decision makers of the impartiality of one's views; as he says, "the rhetoric of authority is more difficult to carry off when the audience is not familiar with the speaker."[8] Whereas before an economist made his case directly to the king or his advisers, enabling him to use any number of rhetorical gambits, in the impersonal forum of parliament anyone proposing a policy could be suspected of self-interest:

As the customary writers on economic matters could not hope to assume the mantle of personal authority and were obliged instead to defend themselves constantly against personal disqualification, to find a form of argument as impersonal as possible was their only hope.[9]

As a result, economists drew upon the two philosophical schools grappling with the problem of consensus in religious, ethical, and political debates – rationalism and empiricism. The former school tried to create a universal language by founding knowledge upon mental intuitions of geometric properties, and from these indubitable starting-points rationalists hoped to deduce conclusions no reasonable person could doubt. Their efforts led to an idealized formulation of the method of deductive science. Dudley North formulated the first axiomatic economic theory, and in doing so was explicit in his debt to Descartes. In the preface to the *Discourses upon Trade*, his brother Roger North stated:

He seems to be of a Temper different from most who have meddled with this subject in public . . . for he speaks impartially of trade in general, without warping to the favour of any particular interest. In the next place, I find trade here treated at another rate than it usually has been; I mean philosophically; for . . . he begins at the quick, *from principles indubitably true*; and so proceeding with like care comes to a judgement of the nicest disputes and questions concerning trade. And hence it is that knowledge in great measure is becoming mechanical, which word I need

---

[8] *The Origins of Scientific Economics* (London: Methuen, 1963), p. 83.   [9] Ibid., p. 98.

not interpret farther than by noting it here means, built upon clear and evident truths.[10]

Empiricists, on the other hand, sought foundations in sensuous intuition, and from here hoped to build up our corpus of knowledge through observation and induction. They thus came to sketch out the method of the experimental sciences. William Petty, the originator of empirical methods in economics, is also explicit in his debt to philosophy, in particular to the empiricism of Bacon's *Novum Organum*. In the preface to his *Political Arithmetick* he tells us:

The method I take . . . is not yet very usual; for instead of using only comparative and superlative Words, and intellectual Arguments, I have taken the course (as a Specimen of the Political Arithmetic I have long aimed at) to express my self in Terms of Number, Weight, or Measure; to use only Arguments of Sense, and to consider only such Causes, as have visible Foundations in Nature; leaving those that depend upon the mutable Minds, Opinions, Appetites, and Passions of Particular Men, to the considerations of others.[11]

Here, as with North, the primary influence of philosophical doctrines is clearly in evidence.

These two examples from the beginning of modern social science nicely illustrate the point that philosophy does indeed play a substantive role in this field. Plenty of similar examples could be drawn from the original tracts of psychology and political science by Hobbes, Locke, Hume, Bentham, Smith, Comte, and Mill. Here again scientific paradigms were inspired by largely philosophical sources rather than obvious predictive or explanatory success. And during this century the positivistic social sciences, and behaviorism specifically, have not been ones inspired by patently successful results, but ones whose methods were often deduced in Quinian manner from prior philosophical beliefs as to the nature of a truly scientific idiom and to the impossibility of stating identity conditions for intentional entities.[12] The effect of these philosophical notions has often been a paradoxical inversion of our notions of persuasive explanation. The locus of reasonable

---

[10] Roger North, preface to Dudley North, *Discourses Upon Trade* (1905), p. iv.
[11] William Petty, "Political Arithmetick," in *Economic Writings*, vol. I, edited by C. H. Hull (Cambridge, 1899), p. 244.
[12] See for example, B. F. Skinner, "Private Events in a Natural Science," in *Science and Human Behaviour* (New York: Free Press, 1953), pp. 257–82.

discussion has been located on the level of methodology rather than at the stage of the conclusions generated. In the looking-glass world of politico and socio-metrics the hopelessly foreign has been used to explain the familiar. The claim on our attention lies in these fields' supposed scientific proof of the point at issue; we are expected to accord the conclusions credence, not because they are credible or even interesting, but because of their method of generation. When method takes center stage as it has here, we are in danger of losing sight of what normally passes as convincing social explanation.

Common sense reactions have occurred when something obvious or natural to our world view or our inherited intellectual equipment is thrown into doubt by a new philosophy. We have seen this with empiricism and skepticism. Today a similar reaction is taking place against methodological views as to the nature of a truly scientific social science. This may well be the legacy of positivism, that proselytizing, fundamentalist movement which attempted to toss the knowledge claims of ethics, literature, history, religion, politics, and the interpretive social sciences, into, in Richard Bernstein's words, "the dustbin of cognitively meaningless discourse."[13] Positivism along with kindred philosophies implied, either from logical, epistemological, or ontological grounds, that there is only one rationally adequate branch of knowledge, this usually being physics. If this is seen as the only science having access to reality, or securely fastened to sense data, or logically transparent, the implication has been that other fields should be restructured to emulate its methods. It is this imperialist ambition of philosophy that has been imaginatively repudiated by a wide range of philosophers since, perhaps, Wittgenstein's *Investigations*. To take as a sample statement of the common concern, Stephen Toulmin, back in the fifties, commented on the "Great Divergence" between rational ideals stemming from formal logic and the actual reasoning practices used by theorists in the front lines of ethics, politics, and the other fields then under suspicion of employing inadequate standards of rational procedure.[14] He wrote:

We are tempted to see deficiencies in these claims only because we compare them with a philosopher's ideal which is in the nature of the cases unrealisable. The proper task of epistemology would be not to overcome

[13] *The Restructuring of Social and Political Theory* (University of Philadelphia Press, 1978), p. 60.
[14] *The Uses of Argument*, p. 166.

these imagined deficiencies, but to discover what actual merits the arguments of scientists, moralists, art critics or theologians can realistically hope to achieve.[15]

Resistance to this methodological pluralism stems from many sources, but chief among them is the persistent belief that ordinary language, due to the vagueness it harbors, is too cumbersome and uncontrollable to facilitate the knowledge that philosophy had hoped to deliver. The distrust of ordinary arguments, ones couched in non-technical terms, has caused rhetoric, which is nothing more sinister than the study of argumentation in fields where deductive certainty or experimental methods are unattainable, to become understood pejoratively as "mere rhetoric"; and the fear that ordinary language is uncontrollably metaphorical and figurative has led to a distrust of non-technical discourse, to what Donald Hall has aptly termed "tropophobia."[16] Consequently, in "our culture" continues Hall, "lethargic prose is taken as evidence of seriousness or sincerity. The heavier the subject the paler the prose."[17] However, the vagueness that the various attempts at an ideal language have hoped to eliminate has remained, like a skeleton in the closet of philosophy. So we should take a closer look at the concerns it has fostered to see if indeed a recognition of its pervasiveness condemns us to a debilitating indeterminacy.

COMPLEXITY AND VAGUE CONCEPTS

The pervasiveness of vagueness is something of a scandal for philosophy. It threatens many assumptions on which the subject has rested, and yet the challenge it poses has rarely been addressed. The *sorites* paradox, for example, casts doubt upon the applicability of classical two-valued logic to the material world. If it is impossible to specify how many grains of sand make a pile, or when the addition of one grain makes a pile where before there was none, then the law of the excluded middle, according to which every statement is either true or false, cannot be applied to a range of statements concerning the existence of a pile of sand. In other words, if the term "pile" is vague, then the proposition "there is a

---

[15] Ibid., pp. 9–10.
[16] Donald Hall, "A Fear of Metaphors," *The New York Times Magazine*, July, 1985.
[17] Ibid.

pile" will in some cases be neither true nor false. In Russell's words, "The law of excluded middle is true when precise symbols are employed, but it is not true when symbols are vague, as, in fact, all symbols are."[18] The positivists' verifiability criterion faces similar difficulties when confronted with vague predicates, for it is not possible to state for all cases what evidence would verify the statement, "There is a pile."[19] Crispin Wright has argued that vagueness poses grave difficulties for the notion underlying much analytic philosophy of a semantic rule.[20] And Peter Unger and Samuel Wheeler have drawn from a recognition of vagueness considerably more drastic conclusions: they argue that our belief in ordinary physical objects is untenable. Imagining an experiment where we remove atom after atom from an object, such as a stone or chair, they ask if there is a fixed point on the atomic level when the object ceases to exist. Since we cannot specify any such point, we conclude, in accordance with mathematical induction, that after all atoms are removed there remains a stone or chair. The absurdity of the result leads them to argue that our common sense notions of objects are incoherent, and that "there are no stones and, by generalization, no other ordinary things."[21] The only language they see escaping this absurdity is that of physics. Putnam takes their position to be incoherent, since the language of physics is rife with its own sources of vagueness. However, he does see vagueness as decisively throwing doubt on metaphysical realism, a doctrine which requires bivalence.[22] Lastly, the gap between the exact language of theoretical science and its application through vague observation terms has lead some, such as Stephan Korner, to conclude that "empirical and theoretical discourse are logically disconnected."[23]

---

[18] "Vagueness," pp. 85–6.
[19] William Alston, *Dimensions of Meaning*, pp. 95–6. He also shows that vagueness poses problems for the notion of analyticity, p. 95.
[20] "On the Coherence of Vague Predicates."
[21] "There Are No Ordinary Things," *Synthese* 41 (1979), p. 121. See as well, Samuel Wheeler, "On That Which is Not," in the same volume, pp. 155–73.
[22] "Vagueness and Alternative Logic," in *Realism and Reason* (Cambridge University Press, 1983. pp. 271–4.
[23] *Experience and Theory* (London: Routledge & Kegan Paul, 1966), p. 63. Carl Hempel argued that vagueness poses a constant challenge to the sciences: "As vagueness obviously is a serious obstacle in establishing hypotheses and theories which are intersubjective, i.e. which may be tested, with the same result, by different observers, it is particularly important to diminish as far as possible the vagueness of scientific terms," "Vagueness and Logic," *Philosophy of Science* 6 (1939), p. 177. Black also takes up this issue,

In short, these examples show that very few attempts in classical philosophy to wrest determinate entities from the Heraclitean flux have escaped its inevitable vagueness.

However, while recognizing that all concepts are vague, it should also be kept in mind that from a more practical standpoint, "the ideal standard of precision" as Black pointed out, "is the standard of scientific precision."[24] Scientific practice may indeed fall short of Russell's ideal language, but when in the social sciences the attempt is made to formalize concepts it is this more worldly ideal that is sought. The choice of ideal is, however, questionable. This is apparent when focusing on the complexity or combinatory vagueness that characterizes many concepts in the social sciences. These concepts, like the word "game" analyzed by Wittgenstein, commonly have many criteria which jointly or individually determine the application of the term. A game may be played for amusement, although war games are not; it may involve the display of skill, but flipping a coin is a random procedure; it may involve competition between players, but the card game solitaire does not. All those practices we call games display many defining features, but they do not display any common one. Wittgenstein called this property family resemblance, and Cornelius Benjamin termed concepts such as these, complex: "A complex term is defined as a conjunction of simple terms, and vagueness arises when we are in doubt as to whether the complete conjunction of elements is required for the application of the term, or something less than this complete conjunction."[25] Alston illustrates the property of combinatory vagueness with the example of religion. There are a number of criteria that can be used in deciding if some institution or belief system constitutes a religion. These might include ritual, prayer, a divinely ordained moral code, an ontology, belief in a deity, and an organization of believers. The problem arises in deciding which criteria are necessary and sufficient to identify a religion. Quakers abstain from ritual; and for some Unitarian and Buddhist sects a supernatural being plays little or no role. At the same time, many of these criteria are satisfied by political or

---

"Vagueness: An Exercise in Logical Analysis," pp. 25–8. Also see the discussion between Alexander Rosenberg and Stephan Korner concerning the former's "The Virtues of Vagueness in the Languages of Science," *Dialogue* 14 (1975), pp. 281–311.

[24] "Vagueness: An Exercise in Logical Analysis," p. 27.

[25] "Science and Vagueness," *Philosophy of Science* 6 (1939), p. 424.

philosophical movements such as Marxism or humanism. The criteria clearly apply to paradigm cases such as Catholicism; but they also leave many cases undecidable, "even" adds Alston, "when all the 'facts' are agreed on."[26] Many of the central concepts in the social sciences are of this nature, and that means that operationalized definitions and formalization in these fields may narrow the application of concepts so drastically that the results of research cease to be interesting.

Wittgenstein's cluster theory of meaning has inspired cognitive psychologists to examine our native practices of definition. Eleanor Rosch conducted experiments into our ability to determine class membership, and found that we do not assign membership in a digital manner, based on a definition.[27] Classes are vaguely defined, and membership occurs in degrees and tails off. However, we do operate with prototypes in mind when using a word. A prototype is an object that most clearly exemplifies a concept, one that displays the largest number of characteristic features: a kitchen chair for a chair, say, or Catholicism for religion. The existence of these prototypes gives the illusion of a defining feature, but their role is not as a manifest definition. They serve rather as convenient summarizing devises. As such they give the appearance of definition to what is essentially a vague concept. They are, as Keynes termed his own concepts, samples rather then generalizations. If these concepts are of central concern to the social sciences then the question they raise is whether or not we can formalize concepts which in important ways have no definition.

This question can be approached through a more general discussion of attempts to wed classical logic with a recognition of vagueness. There have been a number of proposals for achieving this result. Two broad alternatives present themselves. We can try to decrease vagueness in our concepts and retain classical logic. Or we can accept the vagueness and turn to many-valued or fuzzy logics. Quine points out that science is pulled in two directions by its loyalty to system and evidence, and that the simplicity of theory is bought at the expense of links to observation. He opts for the simplification of theory that classical logic affords, but cautions:

26 *Dimensions of Meaning*, p. 89.
27 See for example, "Family Resemblances: Studies in the Internal Structure of Categories," *Cognitive Psychology* 7 (1975), pp. 573–605.

"We stalwarts of two-valued logic buy its sweet simplicity at no small price in respect of the harboring of undecidables."[28] He retains "the law of excluded middle in logical analysis simply by proceeding as if all the terms concerned were precise."[29] Quine's assumption is not as heroic as it may seem if we also accept Rosch's finding that reasoning in natural language employs paradigm cases, because here the problems attendant on vagueness are minimized.[30] Quine suggests this interpretation when he points out, for example, that "typical truths about organisms are true by virtue of certain unmistakable organisms independently of any rulings on vira, embryos, slime mold, and cud."[31] Vagueness complicates the application of classical logic; it does not mean, as Russell had claimed, that it is inapplicable to this terrestrial life. Nor does it highlight a problem with the rules themselves. David Sanford points out that just because two-valued logic cannot deal with borderline cases "it does not follow that classical logic cannot deal with predicates which have borderline cases."[32] Quine further argues that the remaining fringe cases need not tie our hands since legislation as to where, say, a heap or a mountain begins and ends may reduce the indeterminacy caused by vagueness.[33] He suggests that the law profession provides daily examples of this practice. However he does admit that the challenge Unger has presented is in principle unanswerable, and therefore for cases to exist, however trivial, where bivalence fails. He derives consolation from the fact that "notions of austere physical theory remain in the clear. It is only the common-sense classifications of physical objects that come into question."[34]

Black took the alternative course in squaring logic with vague concepts. He proposed a method for bringing vague predicates within the scope of logic, but at the price of complicating it. He began with a measure of the "consistency of application" of a word T to an object x, symbolized by the function, $C(T,x)$. If an m

---

[28] "What Price Bivalence," in *Theories and Things*, p. 32.
[29] *Quiddities* (Cambridge, Mass.: Belknap Press, 1987), p. 56.
[30] Avishai Margolit argues this point in "Vagueness in Vogue," *Synthese* 33 (1976), p. 216.
[31] *Word and Object*, p. 128.
[32] "Classical Logic and Inexact Predicates," *Mind* 83 (1974), p. 112.
[33] Quine provides examples of this legislation in "What Price Bivalence," p. 33; and *Word and Object*, pp. 125–9.
[34] "What Price Bivalence," p. 37.

number of people says the word applies, and an n number says it does not, then the consistency of application of the term is represented as the limit of m/n as the number of observers rises. If many objects are considered, each with its own measure of applicability of term T, then a curve will be obtained running from prototypes at one end to the objects no one recognizes as T at the other. This Black calls the consistency profile for the term. In the middle of the curve, where values are close to 1, is the area of undecidable application; and the slope of this section can be interpreted as a measure of the concept's vagueness. The flatter the curve in this region, the larger the number of undecidable cases. Black then suggests extending classical logic to include this measure of vagueness. Thus, instead of the one-place propositional function $L(x)$ we are to use $L(x,c)$, which says that L applies to x with consistency c.[35] Under this scheme traditional logic is subsumed as a limiting case where c tends to infinity, i.e. where L attains universally consistent application. For any x, it follows that in $L(x,c)$ and $\sim L(x,c')$, the product of c and c' is one. The law of excluded middle therefore can be replaced by an operation permitting $L(x,c)$ to be transformed into $\sim L(x,1/c)$.

Black, according to Carl Hempel, has shown how to replace vague terms by metrical expressions.[36] This in other forms has been a standard strategy of eliminating vagueness: transforming polar property-words such as hot–cold, hard–soft, into relative or metrical terms. "Hard" is characteristically vague; but the relation "harder than" can be more easily specified by an experiment showing that one substance can scratch another but not vice versa. Recourse to this relation thus diminishes vagueness. Similarly, the polar words hot and cold are simply replaced by measurements of temperature. This has been a successful strategy in science, and its appeal in the social sciences is obvious. Polar terms in political life are often freighted with emotional weight, something which might be diminished if the participants had recourse to more metrical terms. Elections, for example, are often fought over whether or not the economy is in recession. The terms recession–expansion, being vague, admit of limitless political debate. Convincing people to replace them with numerical measures of GNP and employment

---

[35] "Vagueness: An Exercise in Logical Analysis," p. 55.
[36] "Vagueness and Logic," p. 178.

could take the heat out of at least that part of the debate which involves deciding which of two polar terms is applicable. Such a view no doubt lies behind many attempts to quantify the terms used in political science and sociology.[37] Indeed, one could argue, if one were a naively optimistic positivist, that the chronic lack of consensus in the social sciences, and political conflict generally, stemmed from the insoluble debates over the application of vague polar terms. Natural language could thus be seen as subversive, the source of political disagreement. If we could retreat behind this veil of words to the numerical scales behind we could, as Leibniz hoped, when disagreement arose, merely say, "Let us calculate."

A prima facie objection to this suggestion is that we already have, for example, plenty of publically accessible economic statistics, the availability of which has not led to the replacement of "recession" by scalar measures in political discussion. This may be due to the ignorance of those involved, so the answer could be to educate people into using a more scientific discourse. Russell, according to Keynes, held the similar view that human affairs were carried on irrationally, and that the answer was to start conducting them rationally. Keynes added that "a discussion of practical affairs on these lines was really very boring."[38] Besides having to impute irrationality to the public, something which then threatens liberal social science from another angle, there is a serious logical difficulty with the project of replacing vague terms with metrical ones. Many of the concepts used in the social sciences display combinatory vagueness rather than degree vagueness, and it is not clear that these can be replaced by metrical terms. The problem can be illustrated by considering the example of attempts to determine the effect of economic development on religious belief and practice. Such studies commonly involve the construction of an index of religious belief and the correlation of this with variables of economic growth. The exercise is purely quantitative, but the results will undoubtedly hide the combinatory vagueness we have seen attends the concept of religion. If we are unable to specify the necessary conditions for the presence of a religion, then the index's

---

[37] The principle may in fact be flawed, as well as impractical. If the theorists of complexity are right about the occurrence of emergent properties and phase changes in social phenomena then the hope of quantifying properties, particularly along a linear scale, may be considerably more difficult than was appreciated by the positivists.

[38] *Collected Works*, vol. 10, p. 449.

technical rigor will be spurious. Alston makes the same point with the example of studies which correlate racial prejudice with degrees of acceptance of oneself: the results "are subject to all the indeterminacy that attaches to questions of the form, 'Does Jones accept himself?'"[39]

It could be argued in response that our focus on the peripheral vagueness is a touch pedantic. The study on religions could confine itself to the paradigm cases, and then the correlation, while limited in its implications, could still impart information. As could a broader study which attempted to incorporate less clear-cut cases; these could still teach us something. Perhaps. But if the question at issue here is one concerning the preferable degree of formalization for the social sciences then it is doubtful that these experiments carry the methodological implications they are often intended to – that metrical terms necessarily contribute to intersubjectively shared results. In fact, quite often the opposite is the case. Alston considers the thesis that city living contributes to psychological stress. Both variables are vague, but if we try to eliminate that attending the word "city" by specifying the number of inhabitants that constitute one, then we arrive at the more precise statement that life in a community of, say, more than 50,000 people causes psychological strain. But we may accord this new version less credence than the original vague statement, since we find it hard to believe that the strain is noticeably different in a community of 49,000. The truth contained in many similar theses in the social sciences does not survive a more precise formulation. Alston thus concludes: "There are . . . theoretical advantages to vagueness. Often our knowledge is such that we cannot formulate what we know in terms that are maximally precise without falsifying the statement or going far beyond the evidence."[40] In many such cases

---

[39] *Dimensions of Meaning*, p. 93.

[40] Ibid., p. 86. He also illustrates the uses of vagueness in fields such as diplomacy. When the United States issues statements expressing, say, strong opposition to the involvement of Russian troops in Hungary, it is an advantage not specifying exactly what is constituted by "strong opposition." The vague statement may keep the Russians guessing, and it leaves open many alternative courses of action to be taken in light of later developments, p. 86.

For an examination of the utility of vagueness within economics, see Amartya Sen, "Description as Choice." He there makes the point that "imprecision of boundaries can still leave vast regions without ambiguity" (p. 353). Sen makes the same point as Wittgenstein that words, or more specifically descriptions, are not picture-like representations of a fact; words and descriptions have different characteristics depending on their

of definition in the social sciences we find that vagueness contributes to accuracy, while precision detracts from it. Specifying a sharp definition of a concept by legislation may eliminate some borderline cases and make it operational and precise, but by chopping off cases of application that are intuitively justified the concept becomes inaccurate.[41] In short, there may be a zero-sum relationship between accuracy and precision. We may define religion in a narrow enough way so as to permit operationalization, but then the concept no longer encompasses all those belief systems and institutions we intend to speak of when discussing religion. In this case of definition, as with other words displaying combinatory vagueness, the undefined word in natural language permits more accuracy in discussions of religion. Quine recognizes that "good purposes are often served by not tampering with vagueness," and borrowing I. A. Richards' analogy of the results achieved by a painter as compared with a mosaic worker says: "the skillful super-imposing of vaguenesses has similar advantages over the fitting together of precise technical terms."[42]

This analysis of vagueness suggests the conclusion that no definition is possible at all in the social sciences. If we are interested in examining religion, say, from a sociological perspective, any operationalized or formalized definition will inevitably leave out of account some phenomena in which we are intuitively interested. Any definition, in short, seems to involve changing the subject. This conclusion comes to resemble a species of the paradigm case

---

purposes. Wittgenstein wrote "What we call 'descriptions' are instruments for particular uses" (*Investigations*, sect. 291) Similarly, Sen warns against expecting any single, correct procedure of description, for what is described will be different for each objective: "any description involves discrimination and selection, and the real question is the relevance of the selection process to the objectives of description" ("Description," p. 357). He points out that the widely accepted view of description as being a passive, picture-like, depiction of reality is too narrowly conceived, for a description can be, in some sense, good without being true at all. For example, we can describe the population of China as 900 million without being accused of inaccuracy; we can, following Friedman, use false assumptions about the world if we are concerned only with prediction; and we can, with Kaldor, employ "stylized facts" if they capture what is significant for us. For both Wittgenstein and Sen description is an activity, and picture-like reflections of facts need to be brought alive by a purpose. Without a purpose, Wittgenstein said "These pictures are as it were idle" (*Investigations*, sect. 291).

[41] Margolit makes this case, in "Vagueness in Vogue," pp. 211–12.

[42] *Word and Object*, p. 127. In "The Virtues of Vagueness in the Languages of Science" Alexander Rosenberg has also argued that vagueness has its beneficial effects in the natural sciences.

argument in that it argues against any tinkering with our understanding of an everyday concept. There is something to this
argument, and it points to the trade-off between relevance and
precision. Keynes's practice is instructive here in finding a way out
of this impasse. He had pointed out the problem in his lectures of
1933: "Many economists in making their definitions so precise,
make them too rigid. This is the danger of scholasticism."[43] In other
words, precise definitions leave too much out of account. But in
theoretical work some sort of definition is required if we are to build
models. "Amidst the welter of divergent usages of terms," he said,
"it is agreeable to discover one fixed point."[44] He took the prototypes as the cases from which to extract a definition for use in
theoretical manipulation. Keynes used the term 'sample' to make
this point, and said that "Generalising in economics is thinking by
sample, not by generalisation."[45] These samples or prototypes he
found in our common understandings, or in the practices of
specialists such as tax commissioners. However, there is an
important distinction between Keynes's use of prototypes and their
use by others who have taken these paradigm samples as the basis
for operationalization or a formalized definition: Keynes, while
directing attention to prototypical samples to clarify his intended
meaning, remained on the level of everyday language when using
the concepts. By so doing he allowed us to intuitively take account
of the wider application of the concept, something that is easily lost
when formalizing these prototypes: "in ordinary discourse, where
we are not blindly manipulating but know all the time what we are
doing and what the words mean, we can keep 'at the back of our
heads' the necessary reserves and qualifications."[46] In this way,
ordinary language can recommend itself on the grounds of economy
and accuracy.

Keynes has given us a novel theoretical argument, one proved in
practice, for the case that the readymade summaries we find
in ordinary language are extremely efficient in handling a complex
subject-matter. He was thus the first to work out the implications
of Wittgenstein's analysis of combinatory vagueness for the
language of the social sciences. This led him to conclude that

---

[43] *Keynes's Lectures. Notes of a Representative Student*, p. 102. [44] *Collected Works*, vol. 7, p. 61.
[45] *Keynes's Lectures. Notes of a Representative Student*, p. 102. [46] *Collected Works*, vol. 7, p. 297.

formalization runs the risk of leaving the subject-matter we are interested in behind. Formalization thus also runs the risk of increasing rather than decreasing muddle. As he had realized early in his career, "confusion of thought is not always best avoided by technical and unaccustomed expressions."[47] Put another way, he had recognized the trade off between precision and accuracy. In his later writings he developed more fully the view that the vagueness of ordinary language was a valued property in simplifying theory of a complex system. His frequent reminder that ordinary language allows us to draw on a vast amount of tacit knowledge displays an understanding of the vague penumbra of cases that surround the prototypes we have in mind. This account of concept formation leads to a very cautious approach to formalization: when, in the name of scientific method, everyday concepts are replaced by more formal ones and the familiar is explained in terms of the unfamiliar, we should be candid in appraising whether the new language leads to a loss of information. Keynes's views thus stand as an interesting response to those of Quine, who finds simplicity in the austerity of his own canonical notation. Simplicity is served by admitting only those entities entering into quantification, a stipulation that precludes entities lacking clear identity conditions. The response we find in Keynes is that without vague terms social theory would be unmanageably cumbrous; a formal treatment that attempts to make explicit even part of what goes into our common sense understanding of an issue can be "prolix and complicated to the point of obscurity."

Today Lotfi Zadeh and the theorists of fuzzy logic share a similar view as to the pervasive vagueness of our concepts, but have engineered a formal apparatus to handle the phenomenon. Zadeh has extended the work of Black, Wittgenstein, and Lukasiewicz by developing a theory of fuzzy logic. He too sees that the world presents us with a bewildering assortment of objects, and that our natural response to this confusion is to summarize the chaos of more or less present qualities by means of words. As summarizing tools, approximations, words do not operate according to the digital rules of classical set theory; they are "labels of fuzzy sets, that is, classes of objects in which the transition from membership to

---

[47] *Collected Works*, p. 20.

non-membership is gradual rather than abrupt."[48] To handle this fact Zadeh proposed extending set theory by permitting partial membership. So instead of having to decide whether a belief system is or is not a religion, i.e. whether its membership is 1 or 0, we assign it a degree of membership. Through a polling process similar to the one proposed by Black we might find that people view Catholicism as 1.0 a religion, Quakerism 0.8, The Church of Scientology 0.5, and Communism may receive a 0.4 membership. By permitting graded membership, he claims, the logical core of the paradoxes arising from having to say when a man is or is not bald, or when sand does or does not form a pile is removed. Digital set theory is replaced by partial membership and no paradox remains. The rules of classical set theory become extended by this approach. Take for example the intersection of the sets religious society and technologically advanced society. Egypt may be assigned a 0.8 membership in the religious set, and 0.5 in the technologically advanced set. The intersection of two fuzzy sets is defined as the lesser of two membership values, in this case 0.5. The union is the higher of the values, 0.8 in this case.[49] This fuzzy logic incorporates classical logic as a special case where membership values are either 1 or 0. Zadeh characterizes it as "a fuzzy extension of a nonfuzzy multi-valued logic" such as that of Lukasiewicz.[50] He believes that this fuzzy logic is the one habitually used in natural language. He claims that its use in engineering can afford us more efficient control mechanisms. And he also recognizes its potential utility in the social sciences, since the concepts we use in political and social life defy formalisation along traditional lines. He too makes the point that there may be a zero-sum relationship between precision and accuracy:

Essentially, our contention is that the conventional quantitative techniques of system analysis are intrinsically unsuited for dealing with humanistic systems or, for that matter, any system whose complexity is comparable to that of humanistic systems. The basis for this contention rests on what might be called the *principle of incompatibility*. Stated informally, the essence of this principle is that as the complexity of a system increases, our ability to make precise and yet significant

---

[48] "Outline of a New Approach to the Analysis of Complex Systems and Decision Processes," *Institute of Electrical and Electronics Engineers Transactions on Systems, Man, and Cybernetics* SMC-3 (1973), p. 28.

[49] See "Fuzzy Sets," *Information and Control* 8 (1965), pp. 338–53.

[50] "Fuzzy Logic and Approximate Reasoning," *Synthese* 30 (1975), pp. 409–10.

statements about its behaviour diminishes until a threshold is reached beyond which precision and significance (or relevance) become almost mutually exclusive characteristics.[51]

Our natural conceptual scheme is admirably suited to the task of summarising complexity, so Zadeh suggests that we move "away from the use of quantified variables and toward the use of the type of linguistic descriptions employed by humans."[52] His own form of analysis however is not strictly verbal since his fuzzy sets permit mathematical manipulation. His variables are, however, what he calls "linguistic variables," variables, that is, whose values are sentences taken from natural language. It has in fact been claimed that fuzzy logic's ability to deal mathematically with vague concepts could permit a bridging of the divide between quantitative and qualitative social science.[53]

Other philosophers, however, think that the development of a fuzzy logic is the wrong conclusion to draw from the analysis of vagueness. Crispin Wright, for one, thinks that there is "no special logic for predicates of this sort, crystallising what is distinctive in their semantics in contrast with those of exact predicates."[54] For what gives rise to the vagueness in our language is precisely the coarse uses to which it is put. In the case of the *Sorites* Paradox, the word 'heap' is only used in contexts where a precise demarcation point would have little purpose. If such is the case then trying to resolve the paradox with a fuzzy set simply misses the point: we have no need of any more precision. Similarly, color words which admit of borderline cases between, say, red and orange, do not need refinement since the way we use this set of concepts assumes that only differences in shade which are memorable are of any use. Lastly, the precise transition point between child and adolescent is impossible to specify largely because the distinction is supported, not by physiological change, but by the moral expectations we have

---

[51] "Outline of a New Approach," p. 28.

[52] Ibid., p. 29.

[53] See Michael Smithson, "Fuzzy Set Theory and The Social Sciences: The Scope for Applications," *Fuzzy Sets and Systems* 26 (1988), pp. 12–15.

[54] "On the Coherence of Vague Predicates," p. 338. Baker and Hacker similarly argue that "It is the final irony, the acme of incomprehension, to take [Wittgenstein's] remarks as stimuli to constructing logics of vagueness or semantics admitting vague expressions, since such pseudo-scientific forms of philosophy were what he was most eager to stamp out," *Wittgenstein. Meaning and Understanding*, p. 227.

of more mature humans. Wright points out that "without tolerance these predicates could no longer sustain the explanatory role which they now have for us. Only if a substantial change is involved in the transition from childhood to adolescence can we appeal to this transition to explain substantial alterations in patterns of behaviour."[55] Wright's view is that a precise physiological determination, or even a fuzzy treatment of the term, would solve nothing, for "It would be irrational and unfair to base substantial distinctions of right and duty on marginal . . . such differences; if we are forced to do so, for example with electoral qualifications, it is with a sense of artificiality and absurdity."[56]

Deciding therefore on when a social science has need for classically formalized or operationalized concepts, for fuzzy sets, or for ordinary concepts would involve understanding the purpose to which its conclusions are put. And answering that question, as explained in the Introduction, would take us far into another book. Keynes admitted that his methodological preferences were dictated by the macro-economic question he was trying to answer. He was catholic in his methodological views; and he did not intend his preference for ordinary concepts to be a blanket prescription for all social sciences. The method we use will depend on the question being asked, and some questions can be fruitfully handled with formal methods. As he had stated early on "There are occasions for very exact methods of statement . . . but there are advantages also in writing the English of Hume."[57] He saw roles for both, and, while critical of the econometric specification of macro-economic theory, recognized many legitimate applications of the method, and was one of the founders of Cambridge's Department of Applied Economics.[58] However, the extreme complexity of historical reality and the instability of expectations with which macro-economics must grapple led him to conclude that this branch of the social sciences is unpromising material for formal techniques. Since Keynes's time these properties of social reality have become the focus of attention of the theorists of complexity at the Santa Fe Institute. They too have appreciated the inability of linear

---

[55] Ibid., p. 337.   [56] Ibid., pp. 336–7.
[57] *Collected Works*, vol. 8, p. 20, n. 1.
[58] Keynes emphasized that the core variables of macro economic theory were not the sort that could be estimated. To do so ruined the theory as a "model of thought."

functions to account for phase changes and emergent properties in social life, and, taking their start from chaos theory, have attempted to construct formal theories of organic, complex social phenomena. This work may or may not succeed in bringing the complexity Keynes identified within the scope of the natural sciences. However, the policy sciences have certain pressing functions to perform right now. So until a fully worked out theory of complexity is ready for use, the need for limited liability in theory would counsel that we continue to follow Keynes's strategy and refrain from severing our connection with the wealth of knowledge contained in our common sense and ordinary language. This approach is, as Malthus cautioned, "the only way of being secure from falling into the errors of the taylors of Laputa, and by a slight mistake at the outset arrive at conclusions the most distant from the truth."[59] For the moment at any rate this is the counsel of prudence.

There is another point that argues in favor of the methodological views developed here, and these stem from the type of political system in which we live. In the absence of a complete system of social engineering the questions we ask emerge from social and political life and the answers must also be injected back into these worlds, in the language there employed. The forum for discussion of the conclusions reached therefore will be a forum characterized by familiar concepts. This is not to say that formalization and technical methods cannot be useful, for the more approaches to an issue the better. In between the question and the proposed answers there is scope for any method conceivable – formal, econometric, historical, tea-leaves and entrails for that matter. But when we emerge from the study or laboratory with our answers we must by the nature of the issue return to a common language, and this must be the language used in posing the question. Credence must then be won by the reasonableness of the theory, by its conformity with our common sense on the issue; it cannot be won by pointing to its method of generation. Rhetoric therefore plays a large role in the winnowing of competing theories; arguments, not proofs, are our medium. In short, much of the work on vague concepts makes it clear that, contrary to the fears of traditional philosophy, a social science drawing on the resources of common sense and ordinary

---

[59] *Collected Works*, vol. 10, pp. 97–8.

language has every claim to be considered a powerful and efficient tool of discovery and communication.

When the virtues of vagueness for the languages of the social sciences are pointed out, much of the distrust of ordinary language latent in philosophy can be seen to be unwarranted – for some theoretical purposes ordinary language is the preferred tool. However, there remain the other reservations concerning common sense listed above, such as the view that listening to common sense is tantamount to fossilizing current beliefs. Common sense may indeed be an inertial force in the intellectual enterprise, but as long as it is not understood to entail a body of timeless and untouchable beliefs, as it may have for Reid and Moore, then the notion merely points to the rational procedure of holding to current beliefs until new ones have fully warranted their abandonment. As Quine points out, conservatism limits our liability. Common sense thus has a role to play equally in the natural and the social sciences. If its claims are more tenacious in the social sciences this is just because few social theories have as yet decisively established a shared research program. Besides all this, my concern in this book, and my immediate concern here, is with the role of common sense in the choice of method and language, rather than with substantive beliefs. And on this issue formal semantics, structuralism, and poststructuralism have offered very little to convince historians and social scientists to abandon their present rhetorical practices.

Marxists and Freudians, in various guises, have argued that what is taking place on the surface of thought is a façade masking interests. But such global judgments founder on incoherence. Lukács's notion of false consciousness and Althusser's structuralism, although admittedly out of fashion, provide obvious cases of the impossibility of retreating to a level of discourse that is immune to the criticisms being leveled against ordinary thought.[60] Marxists

---

[60] Gareth Stedman-Jones develops a powerful critique of Lukács's account of ideology in "The Marxism of the Early Lukács," *New Left Review* 70 (1971). Herbert Gintis takes issue more broadly with marxist use of concepts such as "artificial negativity," "repressive desublimation," and "false consciousness": "The fact that Marxist theory has a language game and conceptual structure of its own, one that takes years of commitment to master and use is certainly no indictment. That there is no substantive mechanism for

and Freudians are not necessarily wrong about the influence of suppressed interests in guiding our opinions. They undoubtedly do warp our views. But this does not mean that the cure is the invention of another language. Putnam's point, made in another context, is apt: "If ordinary language cannot be used to say anything significant, then it cannot be used to invent or justify a *better* language."[61] The exposure of bias takes place within ordinary language, and then as an occasional aspect of criticism, not a permanent rejoinder. That would deprive the point of its point. This criticism of radical structuralism need not be made from a politically conservative point of view as essentially the same one has been voiced by several Marxists, such as E. P. Thompson and Antonio Gramsci.[62] So arguing for common sense does not deprive the social sciences of a critical perspective. Ordinary language is a weapon anyone can brandish. There is a parallel here between the points made by structuralist Marxists and the post-structuralists. Just as the post-structuralists commit the fallacy of arguing from the possibility of the failure of meaning to its inevitability, so I believe many Marxists, Lacanians, and followers of Foucault argue from the possibility, perhaps the prevalence, of distorting interests to its inevitability. The answer to both, as Ricks points out, is that these dangers highlight the difficulties, not the impossibilities, of social and political discourse.

If inquiry in the liberal arts faces difficulties rather than conceptual impossibilities, then the skills required in avoiding the pitfalls amply illustrated by analytic, structuralist, and post-structuralist critics of common sense fall within the domain of rhetoric. But this raises another of the reservations listed above: the belief that without a scientific method argumentation wanders aimlessly. Many philosophers have recently taken issue with this

translating major conclusions from this discourse to that of political life *is* an indictment," "Communication and Politics: Marxism and the Problem of Liberal Democracy," *The Socialist Review* 50/51 (1980), p. 198.

61 "Vagueness and Alternative Logic," p. 277.

62 See for example Thompson's *Whigs and Hunters. The Origins of the Black Act* (New York: Pantheon, 1975). The section "The Rule of Law," pp. 258–69, brilliantly argues for criticism which is "internal" to its subject, and for the meaninglessness of structuralist external criticism. For Gramsci see *Selections from the Prison Notebooks*, edited and translated by Quinton Hoare and Geoffrey N. Smith (New York: International Books, 1971). He there argues that the starting point for political theory "must always be that commonsense which is the spontaneous philosophy" of the people, p. 421.

assumption. The philosophers of the New Rhetoric, for example, believe modern philosophy since Descartes has ignored the successful forms of argumentation that exist in fields where the methods of deductive or experimental science are inappropriate.[63] They have thus turned their attention to the lost study of rhetoric, the study of persuasive arguments. And they have suggested a return to the Aristotelean approach of expecting a different level of rigor and precision from each study. Many of these post-positivist philosophers, and Keynes can be included here, see certainty as occupying one pole of a spectrum of inferring practices, each point on which represents a valid type of reasoning. They see the task of logic as the broader one of analyzing all these practices. As Keynes had said, "if logic investigates the general principles of valid thought, the study of arguments, to which it is rational to attach *some* weight, is as much a part of it as the study of those which are demonstrative."[64] Indeed, some have come to suggest that logic take as its basic form of inference, its paradigm case (although most, such as Wittgenstein and Rorty, would resist any new paradigms), a looser conception than demonstration, such as probability, and make demonstration just a subset of the larger class. Toulmin, for example, takes as his wider concept that of jurisprudence, for he thinks the predominant task in the employment of reason is the weighing up of evidence for and against an argument or claim:

to break the power of old models and analogies, we can provide ourselves with a new one. Logic is concerned with the soundness of the claims we make – with the solidity of the grounds we produce to support them, the firmness of the backing we provide for them – or, to change the metaphor, with the sort of case we present in defense of our claims. The legal analogy implied in this last way of putting the point can for once be a real help. So let us forget about psychology, sociology, technology and mathematics, ignore the echoes of structural engineering and collage in the words 'ground' and 'backing', and take as our model the discipline of jurisprudence. Logic (we may say) is generalized jurisprudence.[65]

---

[63] See for example, Chaim Perelman and Olbrechts-Tyteca *The New Rhetoric*, translated by J. Wilkinson and P. Weaver (University of Notre Dame Press, 1969), and Wayne Booth, *Modern Dogma and the Rhetoric of Assent* (University of Chicago Press, 1974).

[64] *Collected Works*, vol. 8, p. 3.

[65] *The Uses of Argument*, p. 7.

It is the essence of a common sense attitude to these issues to recognize that there is not chronic misunderstanding in the use of ordinary language in the liberal arts. There may be a chronic difference of opinion; but this is not something to be cured by a methodological prescription. It is not even anything to lament. It is just the ongoing process of historical, literary and social interpretation.

Keynes too believed that rhetoric is the inevitable forum for discussion in the moral sciences for here "it is often impossible to bring one's ideas to a conclusive test either formal or experimental."[66] The arguments we make are therefore "exceedingly dependent on the intelligence and goodwill of the reader."[67] Keynes thus emphasized the process of argumentation and persuasion and the meeting of minds:

This means, on the one hand, that an economic writer requires from his reader much goodwill and intelligence and a large measure of co-operation; and, on the other hand, that there are a thousand futile, yet verbally legitimate, objections which an objector can raise. In economics you cannot *convict* your opponent of error; you can only *convince* him of it. And, even if you are right, you cannot convince him, if there is a defect in your own powers of persuasion and exposition.[68]

Keynes believed that in the social sciences we must develop our abilities to thinking systematically and express ourselves in words; and his own "powers of persuasion and exposition" were second to none. T. S Eliot, a friend who had followed Keynes's "growth from intelligence and intellect to greatness" over a 25 year period, recognized his rare achievement in balancing theory with rhetorical skill:[69]

In one art, certainly, he had no reason to defer to any opinion: in expository prose he had the essential style of the clear mind which thinks structurally and respects the meaning of words. He had been both a classical and a mathematical scholar: he had excelled under those two best disciplines which, when imposed upon an uncommon mind capable of profiting by both, should co-operate to produce lucid thinking and correct expression.[70]

---

[66] *Collected Works*, vol. 7, p. xxiii.   [67] *Collected Works*, vol. 29, p. 38.
[68] *Collected Works*, vol. 13, p. 470. See as well *Collected Works*, vol. 29, pp. 35–8.
[69] "John Maynard Keynes," *The New English Weekly* 29 (1946), p. 47.
[70] Ibid., p. 48.

A recognition of the inevitability of rhetorical practices, however, raises the Platonic fears of chaotic subjectivity. The only consolation for these fears is the probability that when a social scientist does talk nonsense there is usually someone else who tells him exactly why he does not know what he is talking about. Such a procedure need not be "mere rhetoric." but then it also could be. The danger is always there. What prevents this, when it does, is not our possession of rules of rational procedure, but an intelligent, well-informed, well-argued audience. In less systematic disciplines than science, such as history or literary criticism, there is no technical method, and yet lines of debate get drawn, and leaders of opinion emerge. I am not convinced that they suffer a chaos of opinions, or that economics is any closer to "scientific" communication, despite its technical appearance. Indeed, in debate with Tinbergen, Keynes made this point by suggesting that biblical studies in fact attain a consensus that can only be envied by econometrics:

It will be remembered that the seventy translators of the Septuagint were shut up in seventy separate rooms with the Hebrew text and brought out with them, when they emerged, seventy identical translations. Would the same miracle be vouchsafed if seventy multiple correlators were shut up with the same statistical material?[71]

In the end, it is not a technical method but a well-informed community of social scientists which is our safeguard against a rampant subjectivity.

A reappraisal of the role of rhetoric should allay some of the philosophical fears that inspired the positivistic social sciences; and it is equally relevant to quieting the fears raised by post-structuralists. Some see the illusion of univocity in natural language as a trap for theorists. The absence of definition entails the conclusion, they argue, that theory will inevitably lead to contradiction. Rather than finding a recourse in science, they recommend a flight to poetics and ingenious word games intended to expose the failure of meaning. It is interesting though that Jacques Derrida and Gilles Deleuze work with similar views as those surveyed above concerning the impossibility of conceptual closure and the pervasive vagueness of our conceptual equipment,

[71] *Collected Works*, vol. 14, p. 319.

but have opted for dramatically different conclusions. Arthur Danto says of the post-structuralists: "Having found discursive language profoundly inadequate as a means of communication . . . these prophets see a rescue in the non-discursive idioms of art."[72] In answer to this claim, Danto quotes Frank Ramsey approvingly: "If you can't say it, you can't whistle it either." The fact that natural language falls short of an analytic ideal, that its words escape complete definition, does not make it a worthless tool. Meaning is not impossible. Once again, our natural condition in communication involves difficulties, not impossibilities. The recalcitrance of language represents a challenge to our rhetorical powers; failure of meaning is always a risk. But there cannot be a global failure, as Davidson has shown. Furthermore, the philosophers I have been drawing on find vagueness to be a contribution to the economy of discourse. In the end it is our rhetorical abilities that determine whether communication fails or succeeds. We are not doomed from the outset, as critics from both formal semantics and post-structuralism maintain.

---

[72] "Vexation of Tongues," *New York Times Review of Books*, September 15, 1985, p. 26.

Index